FACTION MAN

FACTION MAN   DAVID MARR

BILL SHORTEN'S PURSUIT OF POWER

Published by Black Inc.,
an imprint of Schwartz Publishing Pty Ltd
Level 1, 221 Drummond Street
Carlton VIC 3053, Australia
enquiries@blackincbooks.com
www.blackincbooks.com

National Library of Australia Cataloguing-in-Publication entry:
Marr, David, author.
Faction man / David Marr.
9781863958196 (paperback)
9781925203929 (ebook)
Shorten, Bill, 1967–
Australian Workers' Union.
Australian Labor Party.
Politicians—Australia—Biography.
Political leadership—Australia—2001–
Australia—Politics and government—2001–
324.29407

Cover design by Peter Long
Cover photograph by Tim Bauer
Typesetting by Tristan Main

Printed in Australia by McPherson's Printing Group.

CONTENTS

The Numbers: 14 September 2015

"I'm stuffed, aren't I?" Bill Shorten asked the night they toppled Tony Abbott. The Liberals had dragged their battered prime minister from the ring. The new man was dancing. The crowd was roaring with delight. In the shadow of Malcolm Turnbull's victory, Shorten cut the sort of figure Abbott had in office: one who seems not quite made for today's Australia. The deposed leader carried with him a whiff of the Cold War and Catholic hellfire, Shorten of the dying world of trade unions. As Turnbull bestrode Canberra in the spring of 2015 revelling in his power, he presented the face of a modern man ready to lead a modern country. He seemed to offer Australia a fresh start. It hasn't quite turned out that way. The *Saturday Paper*'s Paul Bongiorno reported Shorten's despairing question that first night and the response of an old political friend: "Yes, mate, if it's a contest between you and him. But if it becomes a fight between Malcolm, his own party and the Nationals, then you might be in with a chance."

Shorten was shaken. The polls in the first months of the new regime were humiliating. But he plugged on. The determination of this man should not be underestimated. Nor his daring. He broke the rules by announcing fresh policies without an election anywhere in sight. The factions were quiet. At his lowest last summer, his leadership came under pressure but his rivals never broke cover. As dinosaurs began crashing about in the Coalition undergrowth, Shorten stole from Turnbull the mantle of the modern leader. In the new year he turned the polls around, a feat that earned him, even from the conservative commentariat, a measure of professional respect he'd never enjoyed before. He is still not the man Australians would prefer to be sitting in the Lodge, but by April he had the Labor Party once again nosing ahead of the Coalition in the polls. As the nation waited for Turnbull's first budget, it was acknowledged across politics that a victory by Shorten is not impossible. He is a contender.

Yet even now there's a sense that this is a man from nowhere. Turnbull has lived several lives in the welcome glare of publicity. Shorten has lived only one, much of it out of sight, as he climbed from rookie union organiser to leader of the Opposition. That took only twenty years. He has always moved fast. But his time at the head of one of the country's biggest unions tends to be dismissed as a job he did while waiting to get into parliament. His time as a minister is hardly remembered. He still has a faint halo from the Beaconsfield mining disaster, but he is also the plotter who brought down two leaders to clear his way to power. The sight of Shorten on his phone outside a Chinese restaurant the night of Rudd's downfall in 2010 remains one of the most potent images of the man. He stepped up after Labor's terrible defeat in 2013 without hesitation and to little applause. He was widely seen as the wrong man for the job. He wasn't expected to last. But the polls turned in his party's favour. Up against an unlikely prime minister, Shorten was proving an unlikely winner. Despite the nation's vivid memories of the chaos of the Rudd and Gillard governments, Newspoll, Essential and Ipsos showed, month after month, that Labor under Bill Shorten would be welcomed back with open arms.

By the time the party gathered in Melbourne for its national conference in 2014, Shorten was coming into focus. Mobs gathered on the floor of the auditorium. Emissaries went back and forth. Lone figures hung on their phones. Up on the platform, delegates from the boondocks poured their hearts out about aged care and the latest plan to defeat branch stacking. No one was listening. The real interest in the vast, spring-green Melbourne Convention and Exhibition Centre was not in the fate of equal marriage, or Labor's new brutality towards refugees, but whether Shorten was in control. Pundits predicting his humiliation at the hands of the Left were proved wrong, indeed ridiculous, that weekend. He emerged with a near-perfect score having done what he's done so skilfully since he put on long pants: gather the numbers. Shorten is a master of the art of negotiation, a deal-maker of immense skill. He betrays without flinching. He is hands-on. He calls on his contacts deep in the party. He believes this gives him a better understanding of Labor's thinking than any of its recent party leaders have had. He is not another Bob Hawke sitting above the fray, relying on his lieutenants to bring him the numbers. "Bill is different," says his old mentor Bill Kelty. "He hasn't resigned the factions."

God knows what debts he incurred in those few days in Melbourne: a seat or two for union officials in some state upper house; a place on a trade mission to China; a handful of jobs safeguarded in the suburbs; and out on the fringe of one of the nation's capital cities, someone's daughter to be elected deputy mayor. That's how it works, and no one works the system better than Shorten.

The conference never reached the most difficult item on the agenda: party reform. Shorten can only have shared the relief of the old faction warriors that the hours spent wheeling and dealing over Labor's equal marriage policy meant delegates ran out of time to debate the issue that hangs more than ever over the party: the need to find a new balance between the unions, the machine and the members. Shorten's career is a product of the great conundrum of Labor: the wretched state of democracy within.

When he spoke, the auditorium listened. The ovations he received were not perfunctory. That weekend, his authority was showcased to the nation. But Shorten doesn't quicken the pulse. Nor does he cut a striking figure. Suits don't hang well on him. At factory gates in the old days he delivered great stump speeches in a uniform of chambray shirts and bomber jackets. There's something about the formal dress of the Opposition leader today that suggests a plugger heading for court. He has the great political asset of a big, easy smile. He is learning to look serious without seeming ridiculous. Time and Canberra have taken their toll. In nearly ten years since he came to parliament, he has aged about twenty. In the Ruddslide of '07 he cut a boyish figure. Now there is more head, less hair and not so much of the charm that once swept men and women off their feet. The accent is just right: educated and classless, part Xavier College and part Australian Workers Union. It's a serviceable political package but the question is: can he take his party to victory?

Shorten is grappling with an unfamiliar challenge. Each step of the way on his path to power has been won by deals and faction plays. He's as tough a back-room fighter as federal politics has turned up in a long time. A Shorten specialty is a brutal contest out of sight that hands him a public victory "unopposed." He was the first leader of the Labor Party to win his position in a vote of the rank and file. But that was not an open contest: eighty-six members of caucus outvoted 30,000 members of the party to put him where he is today. But the time of deals is past. An ex-union official and a former merchant banker face the nation in an open contest. Their policies matter and so do their careers and character. Australians are shrewd judges of political character. They want to know who these men are and they bring that judgment to the ballot box.

Give Me the Child: 1967 to 1994

His mother made all the decisions. Ann McGrath came from a long line of Irish Australians. She had two faiths: Catholicism and education. As a young woman teaching in London, she fell under the spell of the Jesuits of Farm Street and determined that any sons of hers would have a Jesuit education. She was thirty and on a cruise to Japan when she met Bill Shorten, the second engineer on the ship. They were very different people. She was teaching at the Townsville campus of the University of Queensland. He was a chain-smoking Englishman who had gone to sea in his teens rather than finish school in Durham. She brought him ashore. When the boys were due, she moved her husband to Melbourne, where he took a job at the Duke and Orr Dry Dock on the Yarra. After the twins were born in May 1967 – Bill was first out, Robert second – she began her doctorate while her husband settled down to run the dock. She was always studying. He was dealing with the men and their union, the Painters and Dockers. He hired them, drank with them, and was remembered as a boss who knew the way things worked: there were always too many men in the gangs at Duke and Orr. But that was the deal. The work got done and strikes were rare. Years later he would tell the Costigan Royal Commission on the Activities of the Federated Ship Painters and Dockers Union: "I have suggested to many people in the past to get a better record you would have to go to Russia or China."

The boys were university brats, parked in day care at Monash and roaming the corridors in their holidays. In time, their mother became a lecturer in education at the university. They lived nearby, in the unprosperous streets of Murrumbeena. She and the boys went to mass each week. Their father never did. Her faith was firm but not unquestioning. She believed in thinking things through for herself. She told her boys to do the same. When they came to her with questions, she said: "Look it up." A new priest came to Sacred Heart when they were nine. Father Kevin O'Donnell would turn out to be one of the most appalling paedophiles ever sheltered by the church. Ann didn't care for the man. She wouldn't let her sons be altar boys. They went to the Polish mass each week. Why, they asked. "Because it's quicker and I like the priest."

They didn't see much of their father. Bill's life was the dock and the men. He was around at the weekends, smoking with a beer in his hand. He took his boys to the football and let them play at Duke and Orr, which was on the riverbank beside the site of the Melbourne Convention Centre. Sometimes he brought the men home. Shorten remembers the union secretary, Jack "Putty Nose" Nicholls, coming round to the house with Pat Shannon, who was shot dead in a South Melbourne pub when the Shorten boys were only six. His father worked with a tough crowd. He never learnt to drive. Shorten says he owes his people skills to his old man. His mother was the brains and drive. She was a woman of incredible determination: the first of her Ballarat family to win a scholarship, the first to go to university. The McGraths, the Nolans and the O'Sheas had come out to the diggings in the 1850s. They were unionists on all sides. "There was politics in her family," Shorten said at his mother's funeral. "Uncle George was a Communist Party member. Grandpa wanted to be but was too scared of Grandma." Ann became a teacher, helped her siblings through university, and then kept studying. She travelled the world and was almost over the hill before she found her husband. There were only the boys. She demanded a lot of them and didn't approve easily. "The breadth of her formidable intelligence should not be underestimated," said Shorten. "Perhaps that was her challenge. She would not suffer fools. She was never rude but she had little time for people who didn't try or who supported unsupportable views, little time for fatuous, superficial humbug. She would be annoyed with people who kept women down. Gossip bored her."

Though De La Salle College offered the twins scholarships, Ann held firm to her resolution and delivered them to Kostka Hall, the junior school of Xavier College, in 1977. Xavier was a school for rich Catholics, but the Shorten boys were not the only ones whose parents both worked to pay the fees. That did not make them intruders. Among the well-heeled clientele of the Jesuits, there survived respect for parents doing what the Shortens were doing: vaulting their kids straight into the professions. "This, from the beginning, was one aim of Jesuit Education," wrote the order's revered superior general, Pedro Arrupe, on the occasion of the school's centenary in 1978. But he directed Xavier to do much more: to turn out "men-for-others." Arrupe's mantra played out in rather different ways across Jesuit Australia. As the Shorten boys arrived at Xavier, Tony Abbott was leaving Riverview, its sister school in Sydney, as a committed warrior in Bob Santamaria's fight against the Red Menace and the collapse of Western civilisation. But

Xavier was a different place. The school wasn't fighting the modern world tooth and nail. Vatican II was accepted.

"Don't let your heads be turned," Ann Shorten told her sons. They did the things small boys do in schools like this: athletics, debating and theatre. In the 1979 Gilbert and Sullivan revue, Robert was a pirate and Bill a fairy. Robert's star shone a little brighter than Bill's. They weren't much alike: Robert was taller, better-looking and darker. His achievements on the track were applauded, while Bill earned praise for his "outstanding contribution" to St Paul's School for the Blind in Kew. By this time, the Shorten boys were at the school's main campus, with its chapel as big as the cathedral of an Italian hill town. Kew was a long haul – a tram and two trains – from Neerim Road, Murrumbeena, but they didn't scurry home. Bill ran the box office for the 1983 *Romeo and Juliet*, played the piano, endured elocution lessons, fenced and played cards: bridge at Xavier but later five hundred. Shorten's love of cards – of bluff and bidding – is a key to the boy and the man. Only in his final year did he outshine his brother as a debater; he was chosen for the state team in the national championships of 1984. Though they finished third, his friend John Roskam was generous in the *Xaverian*: "William proved a credit to the College." None of this made him a memorable figure. His headmaster, Father Chris Gleeson, remembers him as neat and polite. "He was always in a suit, always with his tie done up. He kicked around with very quiet, well-behaved young men. He did nothing of moment at the school. But he was a fine debater and a capable student."

Shorten and his friends gathered round the Roskams' television to watch Bob Hawke defeat a stricken Malcolm Fraser. "We were all very excited by the Labor victory," recalls Roskam. "Hawke was new, fresh and bringing us together. Hawke in '83 was like Rudd in '07 for the young: a fresh start." At sixteen it was already clear Shorten was heading for politics. This was an unusual goal for a Xavier boy at this time. The school turned out surgeons and judges, not politicians. He says his first ambition was simply to be in parliament. He knew he could debate. Though not a natural leader in the Xavier mould – he was never a prefect or house captain – he would not accept defeat in an argument. "The house meetings for this year will long be remembered as Bill Shorten's battle-ground," reported the *Xaverian* in 1984. "His speeches were truly a marvel." The school voted Liberal, but Labor was the only possible party for the boy. Labor was the default setting of his family. He was the grandson of union men on both sides. His mother never turned her back on the Labor world of her Ballarat childhood. And in his final year at school, Shorten fell under the spell of his Australian history teacher. The parents might have been snobs at Xavier, but the teachers weren't.

"I've always been a Labor supporter," says Des King. "I'm rusted-on. But I never saw myself as promoting the Labor cause. It wasn't like that. The classes I taught were fair-minded. I wasn't indoctrinating them. I tried to be balanced." He remembers how smart Shorten was: quiet and smart. There was no bombast about him. King remembers how Shorten lapped up his lessons on the 1890s depression, the shearers' strike, the rise of Labor and the early triumphs of federation. "I taught for a long time and taught a lot of boys. He'd be in the top half-dozen students I ever taught." But what set Shorten apart in that school were his politics. "Bill stood out because he always expressed a Labor point of view," says King. "He always did."

At some point in his final year at Xavier, Shorten tried to join the party. He heard nothing back. So he took himself off to see his local member, Race Mathews, who quickly straightened things out at the branch for this impressive young man. "He is breaking his neck to work for the party," thought Mathews. "He is precisely the sort of young man we want to bring into the party and the party needs." Shorten's membership came through on 3 March 1985.

Xavier left him with an undogmatic faith; a modest swag of prizes; a slight lisp; a close acquaintance with the rich; and political ambitions. At the Year 12 dinner, a drunk Bill Shorten senior fell asleep at the table. It was mortifying. He was drifting out of their lives. Most of the twins' Xavier friends were off to the University of Melbourne but their mother's preference was Monash. She was about to complete another degree there – this time law – with great distinction. She boasted: "I was a very embarrassing mother." Not really. Shorten says: "I chose to go to Monash University because Mum was there."

From the moment he arrived at the age of seventeen, he threw himself into the political fray. He now claims, "I wasn't really that involved in campus politics." That's rubbish. At Monash Shorten became a star of the Labor Right. He was elected almost at once to the Public Affairs Committee of the Monash Association of Students, and had no sooner joined the Fabian Society than he began campaigning to be president. The student newspaper *Lot's Wife* reported:

> Our spies also spotted contenders for next year's Club Presidency, Bill Shorten and Luisa Bazzani, buying drinks for anyone that showed the slightest inclination to sell their vote at the annual

general meeting. We believe that Luisa stitched up John Fetter's vote with a Bundy'n'Coke and four helpings of the main course.

Shorten won. He had joined the ALP Club the moment he stepped onto the campus, and battered away for years at its entrenched leadership. The ALP Club stayed stubbornly Left. When the club put this terrier last on its list of candidates for the new Victorian Union of Students, he outwitted them with the slogan "Vote up the ticket." It's a victory he still boasts of today. Even as a fresher, Shorten was able to pluck out of the air Minister for Defence Robert Ray for an earnest campus debate on taxation policy. And then he reported the night for the student paper:

> In reply to one question as to why the family home shouldn't be subject to the capital gains tax, Robert Ray replied: "expediency, pure expediency". Thank god for common sense in political animals!

Shorten would dazzle students over the years by bringing big Labor names to Monash: Paul Keating, Neville Wran, West Australian premier Brian Burke, and even the prime minister, Bob Hawke. He seemed to know them. More to the point, they seemed to know him. This early meeting with Ray at Monash mattered: in a few years he would become the senator's apprentice.

From the start Shorten was looking beyond Monash. He was taken under the wing of an older student, Michael Borowick, now the assistant secretary of the ACTU. Borowick saw campus politics as a way of feeding students into the youth wing of the Labor Party. "The Socialist Left had successfully used student unions to recruit for their faction the best and brightest of left-of-centre students," he explained to the *Sunday Age*. "So I decided we would do the same thing and establish an infrastructure at a campus level that would recruit the best and brightest of a moderate persuasion." In young Shorten he found an extraordinarily talented recruiter. That was his genius. He gathered a tribe around him at Monash and walked them into Young Labor, where he and Borowick set up a faction eventually called Network. Aaron Patrick wrote in his book *Downfall*: "Network had one primary objective: to crush the Left. The corollary plan, which Shorten didn't spell out because he didn't really need to, was to launch his political career."

Patrick, now the deputy editor of the *Financial Review*, was one of Shorten's converts: "Bill was just the best recruiter there has ever been. 'You must recruit, recruit, recruit,' he would say. 'The numbers are everything.'" Soon Shorten was recruiting across the campuses of Melbourne. His orders were: "Get all your mates into Labor. Go to the conferences. Court the unaligned and the waverers." He never stopped. Face to face he was irresistible. He swept men up in his wake. "If he wasn't fighting you," Roskam recalls, "he was trying to convert you." The two school friends found themselves at times in league against the Left. University Liberal clubs were drawn into these wider manoeuvres. So was the Australasian Union of Jewish Students. The cause of Israel united the Right. Shorten loved intrigue. He fizzed with ideas but moved so fast that other people were left to make them happen. He wasn't great on detail. His brand of politics was fun. "It was about getting normal people into politics, not dour lefties, not freaks," says Peter Cowling, who became Shorten's right-hand man in these early years and is now an executive with GE. "Bill was the life of the party. His key skill was getting people involved. He was 'natural as' talking to anyone. He was charismatic. From extremely early on it was clear this bloke was going into politics and he was going to be senior."

Shorten moved out of home early in his time at Monash. There were rough share houses, great parties and many girls. He earned his way cleaning trays in a butcher's shop. Stephen Conroy was first sighted by this crowd in a grubby house Shorten was renting in Carlton. Jason Koutsoukis, who knew both men, recalls Conroy packing down for games of hall rugby: "A sport where five-a-side teams would battle it out in a corridor a metre wide, trying to get a rugby ball from one end to the other." Conroy had arrived in Melbourne in 1987 to be Robert Ray's lieutenant. A kid from Britain who never lost his accent, Conroy proved to be a master of the dark arts of party warfare. He was only a couple of years older than Shorten. They were wary of each other at first, but in time formed a tight alliance that lasted twenty years until it came unstuck over the execution of Julia Gillard.

Shorten was a figure of fun for the Monash Left. He was mocked as "Private Bill Shorten" for briefly joining the university regiment. (His official parliamentary biography records "Military Service: Australian Army Reserve 1985–86.") Pairing hit songs with campus identities one year, *Lot's Wife* nailed Shorten with Carly Simon's "You're So Vain". Xavier was already being held against him. Derided as a snob in the student paper, a wounded Shorten fought back:

> In your last edition … I was misquoted as claiming there is no dignity in pushing a shovel. This was a vicious, irresponsible and demeaning article. To

put the readers straight I would like to clarify what I said ... I do not believe that the unemployed should have to work for the dole nor should they be forced to do so. Hence, there is no dignity in pushing a shovel or any other work which the unemployed are compelled to do. Hopefully, there will not be too much misquoting of important issues in the future. Having spoken for five minutes I was disappointed to see two seconds of my speech reported. If anyone is further unclear as to what I meant then please see me ...

That winter, at a conference described as "a festival of faction fighting" peppered by "spiteful screaming matches," the Network team took control of Young Labor from the Left for the first time. It was a coup that advertised the talents of Borowick and Shorten to the elders of the party. It was 1986. At some point that year, Network held a camp at Portarlington on the western side of Port Phillip Bay. Out of the blue nearly thirty years later, as he was about to become leader of the Opposition, Shorten was accused of raping a woman at the camp. He denies having sex with her.

Shorten went part-time. There was so much to do, so many new faces to recruit, so many marches to lead up Spring Street. Big issues were in the air:

apartheid, Palestine, abortion, AIDS, famine in Africa. They didn't get much attention on campuses. More pressing for students was the Hawke government's decision to reintroduce tuition fees. Enthusiasm for Labor was hard to maintain in universities in the late 1980s. Shortén managed. But politics at Monash was proving disappointing for him: he never scaled the heights of the student association; a coup attempt at the ALP Club failed dismally; and he was dogged by taunts about Xavier boys and shovels.

He began to lend a hand in Senator Gareth Evans' Melbourne office. Shorten found the Minister for Transport and Communications smart and generous but distant. "I know they say that the Hawke government was drifting by then, but I thought they were doing plenty. I just thought it was really interesting to be at the periphery of how politics works." Shorten was kept busy assembling a database of Labor voters. The Left worried about the civil liberties implications of this novelty. Shorten defended the project in *Lot's Wife* as "legitimate market research" available only to members of parliament. Evans gave the Network kids their only remote claim to a policy success. Young Labor was calling for Sydney's Triple J to become a national network. Peter Cowling had taken up the issue. Shorten backed him: "We lobbied Gareth very hard." An audience was arranged for young Cowling. Evans heard him out. Their part in the ultimate result is impossible to assess, but Triple J went coast to coast. Shorten says: "That was something real."

After John Cain's government was returned for the third time in late 1988, Shorten was employed as youth affairs adviser in the office of the new industrial relations minister, Neil Pope. This was a job. He had a wage. He abandoned campus politics and disappeared from the pages of *Lot's Wife*. Shorten swears there was more to his appointment than access to stationery, phones and faxes to recruit for Network. "No. No. I was a youth affairs advisor. Brian Burdekin brought down his report into homelessness. I worked on the state Labor government's responses. I worked on the youth employment program with Steve Bracks." But Network also flourished. This was the year Bob Hawke came to dinner and Shorten became president of Labor's Youth Policy Committee. And at the end of 1989 he travelled for the first time: to Berlin just after the Wall came down (he has a souvenir chunk), through East Germany and into Czechoslovakia, backpacking – for the most part on his own – and sleeping in youth hostels.

He didn't return to Monash for a year. Network was pursuing an audacious plan that went badly – no, humiliatingly – wrong: to seize control of the small, poor, left-wing Victorian branch of the Australian Theatrical and Amusement Employees' Association (ATAEA). This was not about improving the lot of the ushers, gatekeepers and carpark attendants the ATAEA represented. It was meant to prove to the bosses of the Right faction that Network's leaders were ready for big things in the party. Suddenly university students were working as ushers at Flemington. Aaron Patrick reports them preparing for the onslaught: "They spent a couple of days in eastern Victoria at a training camp working on strategies. Law and economics students from Melbourne's top private schools role-played speaking to poor, older men." The old guard of the union slaughtered the students, and in the shakeout that followed, a good deal of anger was directed at Shorten. After years of infatuation, friends broke with him forever. Some look back to their time in his tribe with bitterness, some with amused resignation. In 2013, Christina Cridland wrote in Perth's *Sunday Times*:

> As a former Young Labor leader said to me at the end of our time in Shorten's Young Labor group, Network: "Young Labor is very good at taking idealistic young people and turning them into Machiavellian mother-------" ... while my initial involvement in Young Labor was motivated by

idealism, most of my time ended up being spent as a pawn for the "king of the kids", as Shorten was known. That is, helping Shorten outnumber the left wing of Young Labor, and even a rival sub-faction of the right wing of the youth party, which was led by Shorten's now close mate and senator David Feeney and another enemy-turned-ally, Andrew Landeryou.

All his life Shorten has left behind people who feel betrayed by him. He denies casting people off when they are no longer of any use. He insists he keeps in touch, even now, with old campaigners from university and the union. But there have been so many new best friends over the years. "You can't keep in touch with everyone," he says. "I get that there is disappointment amongst some people. They look at me and say, well, he's here and I'm there, and what happened?" Many he's dazzled and dumped understand. They recognise that the intimacies formed in political brawls are intense but may not outlast the campaign.

But the complaints about Shorten that saw him walk away from Network were different. Close allies discovered he was dealing with the enemy. Shorten had recruited his followers with a simple appeal to work with his team in the Right against the whole world. But he was looking further down the track, beyond the light opera of smashing the ATAEA. He had a career to consider. "Politics," he says, "is a long-distance race, not a sprint." Some of this was about leaving the amateurs behind and drawing close to the most professional of his rivals: Stephen Conroy, David Feeney and Melbourne University activist Richard Marles. It was a tough but shrewd move. His old friends would happily have gone with him, but Shorten was working behind their backs. That was the betrayal that powered the split of 1990. "We were cheesed off," one explained, "because he was doing it all for Bill."

He returned to Monash to finish his degree. His mother had mandated he must be admitted as a solicitor. That meant finding a perch for a few years in a legal firm. At Slater and Gordon he was interviewed by a young leader of the Left in Victoria, Julia Gillard. Twenty-five years later she wrote: "I enjoyed his cheeky demeanour, was impressed with the spirit of endeavour that seemed deeply ingrained in him and said in the interview, 'We should offer you a job.'" But he found articles elsewhere, for which Bob Kernohan claims the credit. Kernohan told the Royal Commission into Trade Union Governance and Corruption:

He was active in Young Labor ... as an older bloke looking at the young fellow, I thought,

> "This bloke has ability. He's nearly finished his law degree." He was very keen to get involved in my planned campaign in the AWU. I asked Bill if he would be my campaign manager. He was more than happy. In fact, he was relishing the opportunity to become my campaign manager.

Shorten was doing chores for Robert Ray when he fell in with Kernohan. It would prove an unhappy meeting. Kernohan was battling to regain his place in the Australian Workers Union leadership with the help of the boss of the Victorian Right. His solicitor was John Cain, son of the just-retired premier and the senior partner in the leading Melbourne Labor firm Maurice Blackburn and Co. "John Cain Junior talked to his partners," said Kernohan. "They put Bill on."

The young man concentrated, in a rather distracted fashion, on the injuries of working men and women. "From the time he commenced, it was clear his interest was not in personal injuries," says Peter Koutsoukis, who supervised his work. "He wanted to deal with the unions." But he had a remarkable knack. "He was very good at convincing clients to sign up to litigation. That isn't easy." In December 1993, a ten-seater de Havilland Dove clipped four houses in Gilbertson Street, Essendon, before coming to earth in the garden of a fifth. No one was killed. But Shorten recruited seven residents to sue the owner of the plane, Ted Rudge of Rudge Air. Koutsoukis was impressed: "He went out holding sort-of public meetings and going door to door and signed up a lot of people." The case made the *Age*: "A lawyer with Maurice Blackburn and Co, Mr Bill Shorten, said yesterday that the legal action was the largest group claim for nervous shock taken in Australia." The firm settled in the end. "But Bill signed up a lot of people to cost agreements."

Kernohan was accusing the AWU leadership in Victoria of gross neglect of duty. He had Shorten give the details to the *Australian*, the *Age* and the *Financial Review*: "Mr Kernohan said that in 18 years as an AWU member he had 'never seen the Victorian AWU in such a mess.' He believed it faced a deficit in 1991–2 of nearly $1 million." The newspaper clippings were turned into flyers sent to every member of the union in Victoria. In the face of this campaign, the AWU's Queensland boss, Bill Ludwig, installed his protégé, Bruce Wilson, as acting state secretary in Victoria in mid-1992. Wilson was seen as a man with a big political future. But he was grossly corrupt, milking a slush fund he'd set up in Western Australia using money from the construction giant Thiess. His lover, Julia Gillard, had done the paperwork for the fund at Slater and Gordon. The tangled Wilson story would cast a shadow over her prime ministership and leave a permanently disgruntled Kernohan accusing Shorten of failing to pursue the miscreant and his ill-gotten gains.

The young man's time at Maurice Blackburn was odd and brief. "He advised our senior lawyers on how to deal with the media – what should be the angle, what was a good grab," says Koutsoukis. "I remember him going to Channel 9 with some of our senior lawyers one day to advise them. He showed remarkable acumen in this at a young age." Shorten's advice was always the same: "Where someone has been badly hurt or badly done by, you've got to talk about their story." Koutsoukis says he was a player in a great coup for the firm: "He helped us build relationships with unions. He assisted us in recruiting AWU as a client. Bill played a role in that, advising on the politics behind it, and he knew key individuals."

After eighteen months at Maurice Blackburn, his obligations to his mother fulfilled, Shorten looked for a way into politics. By this time, he had come to regard the secretary of the ACTU as his mentor. "He was very young and still a university student," recalls Bill Kelty. "But genuine Labor." What did he teach the boy? "The experience of experience itself." Shorten gave it all a rather courtly air in his maiden speech to parliament: "When I was a young and green solicitor learning about workers compensation from John Cain Jr, at Maurice Blackburn, Bill invited me to join the union movement." Shorten had set his sights on the AWU. Kelty wasn't encouraging: "I told him, 'It's a basket case. By all means go in, but it's going to be a battle.'" The ACTU chief advised him not to be one of those private-school boys who go into unions as industrial advocates: he should go in as an organiser.

"He was very ambitious in all things," says Koutsoukis. "He always had his eye on being secretary of the union and knew the best way to get there was to be on the shop floor and mix with the members. Industrial advocates only get to know the members in disputes. Organisers get to know them all. This was a deliberate strategy to put him on the path to becoming secretary." Even at the age of twenty-seven, Shorten was making no secret of his higher ambitions: "He used to say he would be prime minister one day."

In the Headlights: 8–9 July 2015

Shorten sat in the witness box like a boy outside the headmaster's study. On his face was apprehension and disbelief. He blinked a lot. On the footpath nineteen floors below were the same camera crews that had staked out the Independent Commission Against Corruption when Liberal officials were flayed in 2014 for funnelling hundreds of thousands of dollars in prohibited donations to the NSW branch of their party. Now, a few blocks across town, it was Labor's turn. Shorten's appearance before the Royal Commission into Trade Union Governance and Corruption was early at his request, made in the hope that he could cut through the gathering media narrative of Shorten the corrupt union boss. He swore on the Bible.

Abbott promised a royal commission into the unions if he won power, and they gave him plenty to work with while he was in Opposition. Millions were found to have been stolen by officials of the Health Services Union (HSU). That scandal, still unwinding, left a former president of the Labor Party behind bars. The union's former national secretary, Craig Thomson, was disgraced and fined, and escaped prison only by the skin of his teeth. Meanwhile, Gillard and her government had been dogged by the squalid tale of Bruce Wilson's AWU slush fund and the suggestion that she had benefited from his frauds. In early 2014 the Fairfax press published allegations of corruption, standover tactics and links between bikie gangs and the construction division of the CFMEU.

Abbott announced his royal commission a few days later "to shine a great big spotlight into the dark corners of our community to ensure that honest workers and honest businesses get a fair go." He talked crime but the terms of reference he gave the former High Court judge Dyson Heydon AC QC did not limit the commission to hunting for criminals. At least as urgent was investigating money flowing from employers to unions. These payments come under dozens of guises – some legal and some illegal – but they all cost industry. They boost union power. They bleed into the coffers of the Labor Party and they exasperate the Liberal Party. The search for ways to turn off this tap never ends. Shorten was in the box to answer for deals done on his watch which had won the AWU hundreds of thousands of dollars.

Why were the deals done, asked counsel assisting the royal commission, Jeremy Stoljar SC. And were they done at the expense of the AWU rank and file? "Instead of securing better wages or penalty rates for members, some officials may have preferred to obtain benefits which strengthened the Union balance sheet and which falsely inflated membership numbers."

Shorten had fumbled his response to the announcement of the commission. His rhetoric was all over the shop. He sided too strongly with the unions. He didn't make a firm and early commitment to cooperate. That he was a target was never in doubt. In a profound breach of convention, the incoming government was using its power to investigate – and if possible disgrace – its predecessors and rivals. Rudd was put before the Royal Commission into the Home Insulation Program. Gillard and Shorten would face the trade union commission. As it happens, Rudd emerged little damaged from the former, and Gillard was given a clean bill of health by Heydon. But Shorten's standing suffered the moment the commission was announced. It fell further in May 2015, when Stoljar turned his attention to the AWU.

Cesar Melhem, an AWU official turned politician, was forced to resign as government whip in the Victorian upper house when Stoljar revealed a company called Cleanevent Australia was paying $75,000 in

AWU dues each year while the union was apparently allowing it to strip casual cleaners of penalty rates worth about $6 million. Melhem was Shorten's protégé, his right-hand man and successor as state secretary of the AWU. The deal Melhem struck had been cancelled as soon as it was discovered by the man who took over from Melhem. "I thought it was untoward," Ben Davis told the commission. He ended other similar deals: "I think employers paying membership dues on that scale profoundly weakens us in the workplace."

As Shorten waited to appear before the commission, the papers filled with complex stories not quite suggesting illegality in his dealings as an AWU boss. Abbott was on the airwaves denouncing employers for "dudding their workers as part of a sweetheart deal with the unions." His concern for lost wages and conditions was heartwarming. News Corp's sudden enthusiasm for penalty rates – after decades of campaigning against them with ferocious determination – was profoundly comic.

The Shorten show on 8 July opened with a crowded house of lawyers, journalists, union officials and old political allies. Former ACTU boss Greg Combet sat in as an adviser to the leader of the Opposition's legal team. Mingling with the crowd were beautiful security guards in good suits. We were all safe. Heydon looked almost as ancient as the Duke of Edinburgh. He spoke rarely but with patrician courtesy. His head was often in his hands. On his face through much of Shorten's testimony was fierce disapproval. By the time Stoljar had thrown all he had at the leader of the Opposition, the commissioner seemed exasperated. Shorten had tried his patience. That was clear. But there was something else on that very old lawyer's face that looked a little like impatience with his own mission.

Stoljar landed a serious blow in the opening hours of his examination. He revealed that Shorten had failed to declare $54,742 in political donations for the 2007 federal campaign. After that, Shorten's presence in the box began to seem low-rent. What he had to answer for matters, but was hardly on the scale of the great questions royal commissions are usually rolled out to answer. Did Australia pay kickbacks to Saddam Hussein? Why did Esso's Longford plant explode? Are the churches sheltering paedophile priests? Nothing of this moment was in issue as Stoljar worked over the ground covered by the *Fair Work (Registered Organisations) Act 2009*. Witnesses may yet be brought to contradict Shorten. He may be called back to give further evidence. But in this appearance in the box he was not taxed with committing crimes. Stoljar has accused officials of other unions with corruption, standover tactics and black-mail. He spent his hours with Shorten pursuing conflicts of interest.

Shorten rambled. "There is no way I can answer your question without giving you context." He queried Stoljar's assumptions. He gave stirring accounts of deals done for his workers. He painted pictures: "I don't know if you want me to just very briefly describe a mushroom shed?" He represented himself as an official so busy, so above the fray, that he left nailing down details to everyone below him. He checked little: "I don't micromanage every detail of every administrative arrangement." Melhem was his very busy number two. Employers paid unions for many things – workplace training, advertising in union magazines, paid education leave, tables at union dinners and even union dues – but he insisted that was not evidence of a conflict. The benefit was mutual. And as far as he knew, everything paid for had been delivered by the union. "I would never be party to issuing any bogus invoices, full stop."

The questioning slowed to a crawl. This was by design. Had Shorten's legal team wanted him to answer with a brisk yes, no or maybe, he would have done so. As leader of the Opposition, he was address-ing the campaign against him from the witness box. He was honing grabs for the evening news and educating the commissioner in the ways of the AWU. And like all politicians who find themselves before royal commissions, he was displaying the formidable skill they acquire in public life for not quite – or simply not – answering the question. As Shorten danced around the details of payments of $100,000 a year by Thiess John Holland to the AWU, Heydon stopped the witness in his tracks, put his head in his hands and spoke almost kindly:

> You, if I can be frank about it, have been criticised in the newspapers in the last few weeks, and I think it is generally believed that you have come here in the hope that you will be able to rebut that criticism, or a lot of it. I am not very troubled about that, though I can understand that you are, and it is legitimate for you to use this occasion to achieve your ends in that regard.
>
> What I am concerned about more is your credibility as a witness and perhaps your self-interest as a witness as well. A witness who answers each question "Yes", "No", "I don't remember", or clarifies the question and so on, gives the cross-examiner very little material to work with. It is in your interests to curb these, to some extent, extraneous answers.

Shorten continued, as chatty as before. Rather than growing angry as the day wore on, Heydon grew more polite. Perhaps he'd given up. Perhaps he'd come to think the failings of the leader of the Opposition were small beer. A little before 3 p.m. on the second day, Stoljar sat down. Heydon thanked Shorten. "You may or may not have to come back," he said. "Every effort will be made to accommodate the least inconvenient possible time for you, in view of your responsibilities." The royal commission would be earning its keep.

Shorten held a brief press conference round the corner outside a shop selling ugg boots. He knew the danger he was in: people don't follow the details. They just get the flavour. Whether the commission found anything against him hardly matters. The vibe was there: this man's past is shady. He can't be trusted. The unions rallied round him. Even old foes who might have caused him trouble at this point held off. All were united in opposition to the commission. But the picture was bad. "This hurt him," says Bill Kelty, who watched the live stream of Shorten's hours in the box. "I rang him afterwards and said to him: if you want this job, there is something called pain. To be prime minister you have to absorb the pain."

Billy the King: 1994 to 2006

The AWU was a shot duck. One of the oldest and biggest unions in the country was bleeding members and wracked by internal division. Its industrial clout was all but gone. After a century at the heart of the Labor Party, its political influence was in steep decline. Several state branches were broke. Only Queensland was strong. It was still a 1950s union. What had seemed a useful merger with the Federation of Industrial Manufacturing and Engineering Employees (FIMEE) was turning into a marriage from hell as officials fought over the spoils. And the ground rules had changed. "The old AWU wasn't up for the times," says Shorten. "We moved from centralised wage fixation to enterprise bargaining. That meant organisers had to do more than just turn up in the tea room. You had to bargain. You had to advance. You had to know how you get negotiations done." The outlook was grim and the opportunities for an aspiring politician endless.

Shorten was put to work doing what he did best: recruiting. The union discovered that this young solicitor who looked like Harry Potter in a bomber jacket compelled attention on the factory floor. He was unfazed by rejection, astonishingly persistent and could talk to anyone. These were his father's gifts. Within a year he was boasting that he had helped recruit 800 new members for the AWU. "A lot of people talk about recruiting," he told the papers. "I would like some of the high-ups in the union movement to try their hand at it." Another talent was swiftly apparent: winning the attention of the press with a string of boutique campaigns. The *Age* reported Shorten signing up greenkeepers and strappers; the *Australian* had him leading a walkout of tomato pickers, which threw the 1996 harvest into chaos; and the *Age* covered his campaign to recruit ski instructors in the Victorian alps. The national jockeys' strike of January 1997 made him a minor figure in Melbourne's imagination. Premier Jeff Kennett backed the jockeys. The industry copped higher riding fees. Shorten told the *Age*: "We are all very excited about the unprecedented cooperation between the AWU, leading trainers and the VRC to promote a cleaner racing industry for stable hands, trainers, owners and the public." The Spring Carnival of 1997 was undisturbed by industrial action. The winner of the cup was Might and Power.

At the age of twenty-eight, Shorten was already kicking the tyres of Maribyrnong. He was living in

Ascot Vale, just outside the old Labor stronghold. When a bizarre little scandal known as the Sandwich Shop Affair dragged down the sitting member, Alan Griffiths, Shorten thought he had a show. The Left and Right had been stacking for months, anticipating the fall. Feeney, Marles and a bunch of Young Labor acolytes gave him a hand. But he was effortlessly out-manoeuvred by the man he would eventually dislodge from the seat: Bob Sercombe. Shorten pulled back swiftly. "It wasn't doable," he says. "I didn't have the numbers and I wasn't ready. I hadn't had enough life experience."

After only eighteen months as a recruiter, Shorten was elected to the union's Victorian executive just as Bruce Wilson's frauds came to light. Instead of being sacked, Wilson was paid a handsome redundancy to get him out of the way. The Queensland AWU boss, Bill Ludwig, alerted the National Crime Authority and went to court to try to stop the payments. It was too late. The AWU began to splinter. Bob Kernohan – by this time president of the Victorian branch – was of the faction that wanted to sue Wilson for the money. He would complain all the way to Heydon's royal commission that Shorten was deaf to his plea:

> Shorten cut me off, not in a nasty way, and he said words like, "Bob, think of your future. There's

been a pay-out, we are all moving on." I said to Shorten, "What, sweep it under the carpet like everyone else seems to have?" Shorten put his hands on my shoulder and responded, "Bob, think of your future." He said, "If you pursue this, a lot of good people will get hurt and you will be on your own. Look, Bob, you've been lined up to take a safe Labor seat of Melton in the Victorian Parliament."

Shorten denied this but the commissioner believed Kernohan. "He has had every reason to remember the event," Heydon wrote in his 2014 interim report into the AWU. "He is therefore much likelier to have remembered the event. He has nothing to gain from his testimony. On the probabilities it is likely that the incident took place as Robert Kernohan narrates it." Kernohan's single-minded pursuit of Wilson saw him cold-shouldered and abused by members of the AWU. He retreated from the union, suffered a nervous breakdown and abandoned plans to enter parliament.

Melton was handed to Shorten. After three years in the union he was in despair. He had been on the losing side of a quixotic attempt to unseat Ludwig in 1997. Ludwig survived easily. That skirmish had done nothing to resolve the internal warfare rife in the AWU. Shorten thought: "Do the people here want to spend the next four years fighting each other or are they interested in getting on with the business of representing members?" Steve Bracks was one of several Labor figures who urged him to switch to state politics. Melton was a tough stretch of Melbourne way out on the road to Ballarat. His preselection was announced in February 1998. He rented a flat in the electorate but never left town. At this point he was approached by AWU shop stewards and asked to become state secretary. Deals were done. The cantankerous old secretary, Bob Smith, was shuffled off to the Legislative Council. At the age of thirty-one, Shorten won the union's top job in Victoria unopposed. Throwing Melton away was a gamble. His political future within Victoria was assured: "Steve Bracks said to me after the '99 election: do you know, if you'd stayed at Melton you'd have been a minister?" These days Shorten calls it a road not taken. There are those who remember him reflecting at times: "I could have been premier of Victoria."

Shorten took over as state secretary in the winter of 1998. Officials were sacked. He cleaned up the office. Financial controls were imposed. He hired accountants and recruited young organisers. He found he had a knack for healing broken institutions and managing difficult egos. "I listen to people," says Shorten. "I'm respectful. People don't have to agree on everything to have a point of view which is worth considering." He set about building trust: "You work at keeping your promises to people over time." He calls the aim "relationship trust," where leadership operates not by individual transactions but through a sense of shared values. He culled the union's deadwood:

> You don't necessarily go around with a chainsaw, but over time you set standards and you ask people to measure up to them. Some people decide that's not what they want to do, or they go look elsewhere. You create new currency. You make merit the currency rather than longevity or just a sort of conservatism. It takes a while but it's not an infinite process.

He took the AWU back into Trades Hall after five years in the cold and began to navigate the factions, cutting deals to stop other unions eating the AWU alive. And he was deliberately militant. He stacked on strikes and he won them. Kelty's advice to him was: "You've got to be a moderate union leader. That means increasing productivity. But you've got to be tough. You've got to have a fight." He kept recruiting and within six months was claiming the union had 18,000 members in Victoria. Netballers and chicken farmers were signed up. Every win and every strike was reported in the press. The new state secretary was always available to reporters. He gave good quotes. He honed his rhetoric at factory gates, on the back of trucks, at the end of wharfs. He is still at his most eloquent on the stump.

Soon after midday on 25 September 1998, Esso's gas plant at Longford exploded. Two men were killed. Eight were injured. The fire burnt for two days. The plant was left a smoking wreck. For three weeks Victoria was without natural gas. Esso blathered. Briefed by AWU delegates at the site, Shorten was able to talk to the media with authority. He was quoted everywhere. As he would discover later at Beaconsfield, being the trusted voice in a catastrophe wins public respect. The first profiles were written. *Business Review Weekly* declared this young man a budding chief executive from beyond the mainstream:

> Trade union officials have to be seen as long shots in this selection but Shorten, who is working on an MBA and who spent his early years as a workers' compensation lawyer, has impressed key members of corporate Australia. "I'm the only trade union official in my MBA class, but that won't always be the case," he says. "The union movement needs a range of skills."

When the premier, Jeff Kennett, called a royal commission to investigate the explosion, Esso tried to blame one operator, Jim Ward, for the whole disaster. The commission found Esso entirely to blame for failing to train its operators to deal with the crisis. Ward was given a medal. Esso was fined $2 million. Shorten was all scorn: "Esso makes $1 million a day out of Bass Strait. Suffering fines of $2 million is the equivalent of a corporate speeding ticket for this company."

*

Many women had shared Shorten's life. For some years Nicola Roxon was his partner. He met Deborah Beale in his MBA class at Melbourne University. She was the daughter of Liberal politician and businessman Julian Beale. The pair were engaged in September 1999. She was a futures trader at Merrill Lynch. Her friends vouch for her as funny, down-to-earth, independent and rather more left-wing than him. A few weeks before their wedding in March 2000, she persuaded Shorten to reconcile with his father. They spoke for the first time in nearly ten years. He died a week later.

The Protestant Beales saw their daughter married at St Mary's Catholic Church in West Melbourne at a wedding described in the papers as "a mixture of blue-collar and blue-blood." Marles was best man and Feeney a groomsman. Shorten told the *Herald Sun*: "It's like bringing the Montagues and the Capulets together." Among the 200 guests at the reception were the new premier of Victoria, Steve Bracks, and the cardboard king of Australia, Richard Pratt. Shorten was entering a world familiar from Xavier but he was no longer an observer. He was welcomed. He charmed them. Not least of his recommendations to this crowd was his naked ambition. He had already turned down a state seat and was clearly aiming higher. His father-in-law praised him to the *Herald Sun*: "The first thing on our minds is that Bill looks after our kid, and he's doing a terrific job … He's got what we Aussies admire – drive, ambition and dedication. He cares for people and he cares that people have a job, often at the expense of short-term gain." The young couple bought a big house in Moonee Ponds. Most Australians only know the suburb from old Barry Humphries jokes. But the point for an aspiring Labor politician was this: it lies in Maribyrnong. Shorten still had his eye on that prize.

He made peace with Bill Ludwig. This was seen as a great betrayal by those who had campaigned with Shorten only a few years before to bring down the Queensland AWU boss. But it was a shrewd political move that opened the way in April 2001 to his election – again, unopposed – as national secretary of the union, with Ludwig as its national president. Unprecedented was the decision to allow Shorten to keep his old post in Victoria. For the next six years his platform would be national but his power base was Melbourne. The climb from recruiter to national leadership had taken a mere seven years. He was only thirty-four. *BRW* magazine reported: "Shorten, who is called 'Golden Boy' by his staff, says he wants to make the union function better nationally and to devise strategies, such as training programs, that will make the union less reliant on members' dues."

Shorten's AWU was hungry for money. More was at stake here than the prosperity of the union. Money is power in the party. Affiliation fees are expensive: the bigger the membership, the bigger the bill. The union needed money to recruit in factories and out in the suburbs. It needed money to back its candidates in elections. It needed money to exploit its muscle in caucus. And Shorten was good at raising money. From the moment he took charge in Victoria, he pursued new ways of persuading employers to pay to the union large sums of cash. He was not the pioneer of these arrangements but he chased them with determination and success.

His leverage was moderation. Under the new system of enterprise bargaining agreements (EBAs), companies and unions could negotiate pay and conditions between themselves so long as workers were left no worse off than they would have been under industrial awards. Each EBA had to pass the famous "no disadvantage" test. What an EBA with the AWU offered was a reasonable deal and certainty that it would be honoured. Shorten could set the tariff high – especially with construction companies – because his union was not the CFMEU. A deal with him could keep rogues and stand-over merchants off a work site altogether, or else make them accept pay and conditions set by the AWU. Shorten told the royal commission of a Thiess John Holland negotiator who grew so frustrated with him one day that he protested: "You're asking for so much we could just have the CFMEU."

Shorten struck many deals in his time with the AWU that involved employers paying the union. He insists they were all within the law but won't vouch for the details of every single one: "Whilst I was a very active Secretary, you don't check every clause, you don't line up every pay rate, you rely upon your staff to do it." Some companies paid their workers' union dues. If they want to be members and know they're members, such deals are not illegal. Shorten talks of tidying up these arrangements when he arrived, but he did not end them. He wanted the members. "What profoundly weakens Union organisation is when no one is in a Union," he told the commission. "I make it very clear I support people paying themselves because I think that the more that people directly pay for a service, the more they engage in the quality of it. But in a beauty parade, union or non-union, I guess the union is better." Members are power, explained counsel assisting the commission, Jeremy Stoljar:

> Generally speaking, union membership has been declining in recent years. Someone who can achieve increased membership is bucking the trend. It looks good. Such increasing numbers can give legitimacy to a union's industrial objectives in a particular negotiation or across an industry as a whole …
>
> Increased membership can also increase the influence of a particular Branch or Division within the Union's National organisation …
>
> Inflated membership numbers increase the entitlement of that Union to delegates at the ALP National Conference which in turn leads to greater influence over ALP policy formation, greater influence over membership of powerful ALP committees and, in particular, greater influence over the selection of ALP candidates for political office.

Cleanevent Australia Pty Ltd delivered the AWU thousands of backpackers and students hired to clean up football grounds and racetracks. Stoljar asked Shorten if union membership was almost automatic: "Are you able to say whether or not there was ever an arrangement in place whereby employees had to tick a box on job application forms to opt out of union membership if they wished to do so?" Shorten claimed not to remember. "I might well have aspired to an opt-out arrangement," he told counsel assisting. "But I honestly don't know." In his final report, Dyson Heydon would declare that automatic membership with an option to opt out had been the system at Cleanevent for years. He said this: "Carries a risk of denying workers an informed choice as to whether to join a union. That denial is inconsistent with right of free association."

Stoljar questioned Shorten for hours about EBAs he struck with companies like Cleanevent, companies willing to sign up their workers to the union and sometimes even pay their dues. He was looking for evidence that these companies were, in return, more gently handled by the AWU. An EBA Shorten struck in 2004 essentially wiped out weekend penalty rates for Cleanevent workers. The gap between the 1999 award set by the Australian Industrial Relations Commission and the rates paid by Cleanevent widened even further in the 2006 EBA Shorten also negotiated. Under the 1999 award, casuals were to be paid $33.67 an hour on public holidays, but by 2006 the AWU was happy to see them paid only $14.24. In the witness box of the royal commission, Shorten insisted that that was the going rate for casual cleaners in the real world:

> If you and I, in 2004 or 2005, were to go out to a fairground or a dog track or a racetrack and find everyone there receiving double time and a half plus a casual loading, to me is fanciful in the real world ... it would be great if everyone was getting the Rolls Royce rates which you are asserting, but I have to say in the real world that evidence isn't there.

Heydon would heap scorn on that reasoning in his final report:

> If it was the case that there was a general practice of employers in the event cleaning industry to fail to pay workers their award entitlements, it is a very odd course for a union to assist in continuing that practice. Award entitlements cannot be treated as "gold standard." They are the minimum conditions to which workers are entitled. Moreover, the

1999 award was an enterprise award obtained spe-
cifically for Cleanevent's employees.

Heydon was most concerned that both the company
and the union had "side-stepped the scrutiny of the
Australian Industrial Relations Commission" by not
declaring those pay gaps when registering the 2004
EBA. Shorten acknowledged – and regretted – that the
commission was not alerted. In his final report, Heydon found that as a result of the commission being
"presented with misleading statutory declarations ...
Cleanevent employees were deprived of one of the
important protections afforded to them under the
industrial legislation at the time." In 2015 the present
leadership of the AWU had the Cleanevent EBA cancelled arguing that it was contrary to the public interest.
The AWU assured Fair Work Australia it would be
"highly unlikely that any employee would have any
objections to the agreement being terminated."

Shorten knew how to raise cash. He persuaded
the Packer family's Consolidated Press to smarten
up the *Australian Worker* and sell it on newsstands.
Among stories of fresh awards, job threats, historic
achievements and tributes to retiring organisers, the
Women's Weekly of the union movement carried big
ads for super funds, Maurice Blackburn and employers of AWU labour. "Nothing untoward about that,"

Shorten told the commissioner. "Unions have been asking employers and supporters of employers to put ads in their union journals since union journals were printed."

One of Shorten's happiest inventions was the annual AWU ball at Crown Casino in Melbourne. Officially black tie, it brings 800 or so union delegates together for a swanky night of splendid food, big-name comedians and political grandstanding in the Palladium ballroom. Gough Whitlam addressed one of the early shindigs. "This is," he remarked in his sombre drawl, "a long way from the shearing shed." Each year, Labor premiers and prime ministers, presidents of the ACTU, treasurers and MPs gathered in what came to seem, more and more, an act of homage to Shorten, the new man of the Labor Right. Here was the kicker: employers paid for it all. "If the company is willing to pay for its delegates and their partners to get dressed up and have a night out, again, I don't see anything untoward," Shorten told the commission. "Quite frankly, I wouldn't be doing my job if I was asking workers to pay for their own tickets."

A North American innovation saw a river of cash flow into the AWU. "It was the idea of a levy," Shorten explained to the commission, "a paid education levy, which would be provided by the company, some small per capita nominal amount which could be used for the training of employees and workers to improve the quality of workplace relations." In 2001, the AWU was asking employers for five cents for every hour worked by each union member. The companies pushed back. "I had a lot of trouble necessarily going to employers getting them to agree to this," confessed Shorten. "Some employers were happy to pay just for user paid services. Some employers didn't want to pay for any training and would resist it. Some were happy to come to seminars, and I did get a few to have paid education."

Over three glorious years from 2003, glassmaker ACI, the chemical giant Huntsman International, Chiquita Mushrooms, glassmaker Potters Industries, cleaning supplier Cognis Australia and concrete reinforcing company Ausreo Pty Ltd handed over a total of $650,000 that appeared in the AWU's books as "paid education leave." Shorten assured the commission the money was spent on training, that the payments were not secret. He was making speeches extolling paid education leave and delegates, he said, could see the benefits in the workplace. Though usually struck during EBA negotiations, Shorten insisted the deals did not raise conflicts of interest. "The best way you create sustainable companies, which is therefore in the best interests of their employees, is you improve productivity, or, put more bluntly, it's when you can try and find a win/win in industrial relations."

Heydon would tear into Shorten's argument. His commission paid particular attention to the biggest of the deals, one that saw ACI pay the union $160,000 a year for three years at a time that the glassmaker was introducing changes in its factories that disadvantaged AWU members. There was nothing about paid education leave in the EBAs registered by the union and ACI in these years. Indeed, the deal was never documented at all nor were the payments disclosed to union members employed by ACI. The glassmaker drew the cheques from a Westpac account used to make confidential or sensitive payments. Only one cheque butt referred to paid education leave. All this left Heydon deeply suspicious:

> The payments were made in the absence of any written agreement or indeed any supporting documentation other than invoices. That payments of this size would be made in these circumstances suggests that the reasons why the parties were not prepared to document the true basis of the arrangement was that they were concerned that it was not a legitimate one.

Always the ideas man, Shorten stood above the messy – and, Heydon claimed, potentially criminal – details of the scheme's implementation. The commissioner would accept that Shorten had no "substantial involvement" in the deal struck with ACI. He didn't send the invoices. Once again, the paperwork was left to his sidekick Cesar Melhem.

And how did the AWU spend this river of cash? "Anything that we raised in terms of paid education was always spent for education and training of members," claimed Shorten. Heydon curtly dismissed that claim: "Payments for paid education leave, of any kind, were simply treated as part of the union's general revenue." The minutes of the Victorian branch committee meetings record no discussions about how the new wealth was to be spent. Following the paper trail, the commission discovered about half the revenue was "deposited into the AWU long service leave account and monies from that account were lent to the AWU national office to pay down a loan related to the renovation of the Victorian Branch and National Offices."

*

Standing in an empty paddock on Ferntree Gully Road, heckled by protesters, Steve Bracks turned the first sod for the biggest city road project in the nation. For thirty years, planners had wanted to run a freeway down from the eastern suburbs of Melbourne to Frankston on Port Phillip Bay. Bracks had quashed the idea when he came to office; revived it; faced down fears about birds and wetlands; reneged on a promise not to have tolls; and awarded the project to a consortium that included construction giants Thiess and John Holland. The 45-kilometre freeway plus spaghetti junctions would cost $2.5 billion and take three years to build. At the sod turning in March 2005, Bracks named the project EastLink.

The AWU's EBA with Thiess John Holland was registered a few days before the ceremony. Shorten negotiated it personally. The deal had been reported widely in the Melbourne press. "Tollway workers to earn $100,000" was the headline in the *Age*. Wages would rise 14 per cent over three years. Construction would continue through weekends, with employees able to choose when to take rostered days off. The consortium was happy. Shorten was proud. An angry CFMEU tried and failed to have the Australian Industrial Relations Commission bust the deal. "It was a big proposition," Shorten told the royal commission. "I was very interested in terms of making sure we got the best possible deal for the AWU workers on that site. Once I'd done that, then organisers and delegates and other people would get in behind that and do a lot of the day-to-day work of the Union representing its members."

Two months after Bracks dug that sod, the AWU issued the first of a series of invoices which would see Thiess John Holland pay the union exactly $100,000 plus GST in each of the three years it took to build the road. This part of the deal was neither canvassed in the *Age* nor mentioned in the EBA. It was concealed from Thiess John Holland executives, never put in writing and never revealed to the men and women of the union building EastLink. Heydon would find "no suggestion that the agreement was disclosed to the AWU members at any stage of the project."

The deal, which delivered $300,000 to the AWU, seems to have grown from a proposal Shorten made early in the EBA negotiations that Thiess John Holland help the union hire a dedicated organiser for the project. Shorten's memory of the negotiations was terribly vague but he thought he would have discussed how the AWU could maintain an active presence on EastLink: "That would and could have involved services being delivered by the AWU to make sure we had an engaged membership on the site." Heydon thought the magic figure of $100,000 per year was probably decided a little further down the track in talks between the consortium and Melhem. By this time the idea of a dedicated organiser appears to have evaporated and the parties set out a completely different basis for the "agreed sum":

AWU ball   50 @ 125 = $6,250
Australian Worker   4 @ 7500 = $30,000
Sponsorship of AWU OH&S conference 12/8/2006
$25,000
OH&S training for HRS reps on EastLink
$38,750
Total $100,000.

Each year the cost of ball tickets, ads and training tallied precisely $100,000. The figures were comic but both the union and the consortium did their best to insist genuine services were delivered to Thiess John Holland. Shorten distanced himself from the paperwork: "I cannot speak to invoices specifically issued after my time and, indeed, invoices issued during my time." But he was certain that in his day services the union charged for "could always be explained by reference to functions performed, for training delivered, and this is entirely sensible workplace relations." Stoljar queried a $30,000 plus GST charge to the consortium in early 2006 for "research work done on Back Strain in Civil Construction Industry." Was that work done?

SHORTEN: Back strain ... is a huge issue in civil construction and heavy industry.

STOLJAR: I wasn't asking whether it was a huge issue. What I am asking you is, in the period leading up to 18 January 2006, was research work done by the AWU Vic. in relation to back strain?

SHORTEN: I can't say, I don't recall it, but I believe it would have been if the invoice is issued.

STOLJAR: Well, the Royal Commission has issued a notice-to-produce seeking records relating to this research to the AWU Vic. and nothing has been produced.

SHORTEN: If that's what's happened, that's what's happened.

STOLJAR: Well, does that suggest to you that if any research was done, it didn't culminate in a report or the like?

SHORTEN: No. It just suggests to me that the AWU can't find the research.

Heydon would conclude that the AWU issued a number of false invoices for services never performed – including back strain research. None of the invoices was signed by Shorten. So what were these payments really for, asked Heydon:

> They were no more than large donations made
> upon the solicitation of Cesar Melhem. They must
> inevitably have weakened the AWU's bargaining
> position, both in relation to the 2005 EBA and in
> relation to the AWU's engagement with the work-
> ers on the Eastlink site over the life of the project.
> They compromised the AWU's capacity to repre-
> sent the interests of its members when it came to
> industrial relations issues that may arise on site.
> That is because the relevant organisers and offi-
> cials were effectively in the pay of the employers.

Shorten continues to boast that the EastLink EBA
was "a very good agreement" and those $100,000
payments each year were another of the win/win
deals brokered by the AWU. The invoices continued
to be issued and paid well after Shorten handed the
state presidency of the union to Melhem. By the time
they ceased, EastLink was open for business – under
budget and well ahead of schedule – and Bill Shorten
was in parliament.

Let It Zing: 2014 to …

One night I watched Shorten on the stump at the Sussex Street headquarters of the NSW Labor Party. It was cold in the courtyard. Old union banners hung from the walls. There was beer and champagne. Faction heavies had gathered for the event. Senator Kim Carr of Victoria was there, patrolling the shadows like the headmaster he might have been had he stuck to teaching. Standing at a microphone in the gloom, Shorten let them have it. He was good:

> I believe that Australians are hungry for greater meaning, for a bigger story than fear of the future, fear of the unknown, fear of the different. Australians are smart and they should not be underestimated by this current government. Australians are now organising their lives for this marvellous twenty-first century we live in. They are preparing for the big shifts …

These were his people and he spoke to them with the passion of a revivalist. He knows he does this well. But he seems to mistrust eloquence that comes so easily. He distrusts his union voice. He's taken coaching from time to time since becoming leader. He wants to sound different. "I was a union speaker for fourteen years but I've got to have more styles than just that," he says. "It's not about changing the substance. You've got to take some of the rabble-rouser out of you. I think it's about making what you say accessible to people, and people won't always want one gear in a speaker, they want a range of gears."

He can do a fine set speech. His budget replies in both 2014 and 2015 did their work. But so often his efforts are laboured. His big vocal gestures are forced. He can't act. When he strives for significance it doesn't come off. And waiting to pounce is Shaun Micallef. "A lot of what he says has an imposed gravity," says the leader of the *Mad as Hell* team. "It's as if he's closing the book and declaring the conversation is at an end. But it's not quite the final word it needs to be, to be the final word."

Mad as Hell broadcast the first Shorten "Zinger" in September 2014. "It was my co-writer Gary McCaffrie's idea to give what Bill says the shape of a Zinger," says Micallef. "Some were jokes and attempts at epigrams we stumbled across on YouTube or on the news. There was a really nice one likening the budget to the Titanic with barnacles that had to be scraped off before the ship could be relaunched – the Titanic, relaunched? Barnacles?

"There was a grab of him on a loudspeaker in Adelaide shouting about submarines," recalls Micallef. "Give it a hard cut at the end and it sounds like a joke. You can do that with almost anything he says. He speaks with a cadence that suggests a set-up and a punchline. It has the grammar of a joke but they really aren't jokes. Gary thought of providing the box for them – the intro and the outro – to give what Bill says the shape of a Zinger. He thought it would be nice to end with a hard cut and a lion's roar ... It became a thing."

I'D LIKE TO TEACH THE WORLD TO ZING

ANNAPURNA HIEROGLYPH: That the Titanic was never rebooted or de-barnacled doesn't get in the way of that being a fucking classic. But jokes like that don't write themselves; believe it or not, someone actually thinks them up.

Cut: interior of room – day. Bare except for a desk with computer, a chair and a whiteboard. Pictures of Oscar Wilde, Noel Coward, George Bernard

Shaw, Groucho Marx and Kathy Lette line the wall. A writer, Simon Frotting, talks to Annapurna as they watch an old small portable TV (TV's back to us).

ANNAPURNA (*voice over*): This is former *Full Frontal* writer and now current chief speechwriter for Bill Shorten, Simon Frotting.

The audio from the TV he's watching can be heard.

SHORTEN: Once upon a time I thought denial was a river in Egypt. It's actually the attitude of the Abbott government.

SIMON (*looking up pleased*): That's one of mine.

Jump-cut through some shots of Simon typing, sitting at his desk bouncing a ball off the wall and catching it, opening a Xmas cracker and reading the joke (which he likes and writes down).

ANNAPURNA (*voice over*): Simon spends up to thirteen hours a day crafting his boss's Joke For The Day. Simon also doubles as Labor's head of policy development, so he has plenty of time on his hands.

Cut: Simon at whiteboard, where we see a number of scrawled sentences. Simon takes Annapurna through these.

SIMON: OK, so we've got a couple of examples here: "Tony Abbott: beautiful one day, gone the next." That's if Abbott happens to be in Queensland when the leadership spill happens ... and a variation: "This lame duck just had his goose cooked."

Annapurna smiles politely; Simon is defensive.

ANNAPURNA: From a barely thought-out idea scrawled on a whiteboard to the ears of thousands of Labor voters all over Australia, we see the awesome power of words ... (*She wanders off on a walk, across the path of Shaun at his desk.*) ... words delivered almost but not quite in the right order and sometimes even mispronounced or left out entirely. True satire then is about challenging the paradigm and changing minds, not about silly made-up character names. (*beat*) Annapurna Hieroglyph for *Mad as Hell*.

Politicians often come to speak like their leaders. Blame osmosis. From the other side of the House,

Malcolm Turnbull watched the Labor front bench master the art of delivering the Zinger:

> It is like a bit of chewing tobacco. They roll it up against the top of their mouths, they roll it around their cheeks, their pupils dilate, there is a straining expression reminiscent to anyone who has had experience with young children and then – boom! – out it comes! A literary Exocet aimed at the heart of your victim!

Aficionados collected lists of Shorten's best efforts. Widely regarded as among the finest are:

> These people opposite are the cheese-eating surrender monkeys of Australian jobs.

> Treasurer Hockey … should just go down to Bunnings, not Bunnings, go to Kmart or Target, buy himself a white tea towel, put it on a wooden broom and wave surrender on his silly changes.

> If I can borrow from *The Castle*'s line: if anyone thinks that Tony Abbott did this because he cares about the health system and he won't try again, tell 'em they're dreamin'.

We have now arrived at a situation where Tony Abbott's more likely to visit Greenland than Queensland.

In March 2015 *Mad as Hell* was nominated for a Logie in the category Most Outstanding Light Entertainment Program. It was up against *The Voice* but hopes in the Micallef camp were high. They approached Shorten, who agreed to pre-record an acceptance speech. He wrote the words. Micallef directed the shoot. They pulled it off in a single take.

An office. Day. The leader of the Opposition is flanked by flags.

SHORTEN: Hello, everyone. As an unofficial member of the *Mad as Hell* cast, I take great pride in accepting this award on behalf of the show. Frankly, I'm as surprised as you it won. I much prefer some other show whose name I just can't remember. But when Shaun first approached me and the other writers about this project we had no idea how successful we were going to be.

He is handed a Logie. His expression is unflinching, a mix of triumph and hurt pride.

So, thank you. I'm going to keep this for myself. I don't see why I should give it to Shaun Micallef. After all, I've been writing half of his material. And anyway he has been giving it to me for the last couple of years.

Lion's roar.

And the winner was … *The Voice.*

Shorten is still at it, says Micallef. "But there are fewer now. We struggle to find them. I don't flatter myself that I'm responsible for this." Will *Mad as Hell* continue to put Zingers to air? "If they are given to us, it is our duty to continue. But it's up to Bill, not up to us."

Brutal Maths: 2000 to 2006

"If you finally think you understand it, you've really missed the point."

— IRISH SAYING

They found Greg Wilton dead in his car at 9 a.m. on a remote road in the bush. The Commodore was running. Its lights were on. After a terrible couple of months, the Labor member for Isaacs had killed himself. His marriage collapsed when he was sprung having an affair in Canberra. Weeks later, he was disturbed in another stretch of Victorian bush with his kids in the car, rigging a hose to the exhaust. Police were considering charges. It was all over the papers. He checked himself into a psychiatric hospital in Geelong, but left to live with his sister. She insists the last straw was an article in the *Herald Sun* reporting the manoeuvres already underway in his faction to dump him: "And the last words that Greg said … were about his so-called mates in the

ALP desperately trying to take his job off him." Wilton drove alone into the Yarra Ranges, found a spot on the Tea Tree Track and reconnected the hose. This time it worked.

After a day of tearful condolence speeches in Canberra celebrating Wilton's knockabout virtues and the perils of public life, faction warfare erupted in Victoria. They do politics differently there. Wars are fought in the name of peace. Explosives are packed under the foundations of the Labor Party in the name of stability. They call the wreckage left after these brawls rejuvenation. The wonder is that Victoria delivers any Labor talent to Canberra and remains, decade after decade, a stronghold of the party. Long before Wilton's death in the winter of 2000, the factions had ceased fighting over policy. All that was at stake in the conflicts that had shaken the party for over a decade were places in parliament. In no other party and no other state has so much political blood been spilt for half a metre of leather. Unexpected preselection contests are the most vicious. The conflict is swift and brutal. In caucus, Stephen Conroy was blamed for planting that *Herald Sun* story to promote the candidate he, Shorten and Feeney wanted for Isaacs. Conroy denied the charge. "How low can these animals go?" Mark Latham wrote in his diary the day of Wilton's funeral. "Hounding a bloke already in deep shit."

Shorten didn't invent the system. He mastered it. In the early years of the new century he came to learn everything he needed to know about courtship and betrayal, deals and numbers, to make him a power in the factions. If he were ever to become Labor leader, he had to turn the machinery to his advantage. The war in the Right that began over Isaacs would see the factions in Victoria splinter; put the careers of Steve Bracks and Kim Beazley into play; distract Labor in two federal campaigns; and end with Shorten's translation to Canberra. It was tough. He suffered at this time some of the few setbacks of his career. But these were the years in which he consolidated his authority in Victoria and the party beyond. The player became the master of the factions. He still is.

A little history: first there was the Split and then the Intervention. "It was the beginning of a golden age for Labor in Victoria," recalls Race Mathews, now retired to his books in a house by the Yarra. "Those were good years to be in the party if you were serious about politics. Victoria leaned more Left than the rest of Australia, but the Left had no hegemony. It was a very lively and interesting party where the grassroots mattered, where there were spirited debates in the branches and party conferences." But the new rules that came with Whitlam's intervention in 1970 had a downside: "The formation of the factions."

Officially there were three: Labor Unity on the right, the Independents in the middle and the old trade union push rebranded the Socialist Left. The labels are confusing: Labor Unity was a byword for bitter division, and the Socialist Left had abandoned socialism and its old dream of bringing down capitalism. Those dreams had lingered into the 1980s, when Hawke persuaded his bitter enemies in the party to back the Prices and Incomes Accord and then – under threat of a second intervention – compelled Labor in Victoria to allow the return of the big unions that departed with the Split. Their arrival at the 1985 state conference of the party at Coburg Town Hall, with the president of the Musicians Union up in the gallery playing the last post on his clarinet, was a magnificent occasion: "As right-wing delegates arrived at the conference they were met by screaming abuse, jostled, punched and pelted with tomatoes. The brawling continued into the conference hall with some delegates scuffling on the floor and tomatoes being hurled across the room … scuffles, screaming and tomato throwing continued as party officials struggled to maintain order."

That was the year young Bill Shorten joined the party. With rank-and-file membership falling away, the manoeuvres of the factions were becoming more urgent. Rules introduced to bring democracy to the party fifteen years earlier were being gamed expertly by both sides. Branch stacking was rife through the Labor suburbs. The Svengali of the Right was portly senator Robert Ray, whose chief lieutenant was Stephen Conroy. Andrew Clark analysed the art of Conroy in the *Financial Review*:

> His opponents use words like thuggish and bullying, but Conroy adopted a Stakhanovite approach to the task of factional organisation. He soon dominated Labor branches in the seat of Gellibrand, then spread his influence throughout the state. Conroy was not an originator, but he quickly honed the skills required in the brutal world of factional politics: recruiting new faction-friendly members in key branches, cutting deals across factional lines, flattering waverers, shoring up allies and intimidating enemies.

The bonding of Conroy and Shorten in the 1990s shifted the plates under Victorian politics. Together with David Feeney, by this time state secretary of the party, and Richard Marles, who had become ACTU assistant secretary, the men formed a new subfaction called the ShortCons. It has had – and continues to have – a big impact on national politics. In the late 1990s, this band of brothers set about winning a cut of the spoils in Victoria at the expense of the smooth old warrior who ran Labor Unity for years. The struggle between Greg Sword and the ShortCons broke into open warfare when a candidate had to be found to replace poor Greg Wilton in Isaacs.

Sword was boss of the National Union of Workers. He was the great pioneer of fundraising from employers. The NUW was cashed up and well organised. It had clout. Then along came Shorten, whose revival of the AWU threatened the place of the NUW in the industrial scheme of things as the big, tough but sensible, blue-collar union. "They were the industrial pack leaders," says Shorten. That was until he came along. "I think in my time at the AWU the space wasn't filled by just one union on the Right side of Labor politics." The rivalry of the leaders was intense. Some speak of hatred between them. According to the press at the time, when Sword found the ShortCons pushing their own candidate for Isaacs, he threatened to have Feeney sacked. Sword is said to have told Conroy: "If the NUW is going to be fucked over, if there is going to be a war between us, then David will be the first casualty." The ShortCons blinked. They agreed to back Sword's candidate. But so public had this stoush become that the national executive of the party intervened and Isaacs was given to a local woman with no factional backing, Ann

Corcoran. Hers was to be a short career in Canberra. A false peace was brokered within Labor Unity that saw Sword elected national president of the ALP. He was already state president. Shorten was the favourite to succeed him.

Power in Victoria meant finding allies on the other side of the aisle. Unlikely alliances were key to the mastery of the factions. Shorten was courting the "new militants" of the union movement, led by a rabble-rouser called Craig Johnston, whose specialty was leading raiding parties of balaclava-clad unionists through factories and offices. In Bendigo one of these "run-throughs" saw the tires of every car in the factory carpark slashed. At Skilled Engineering in Box Hill in the winter of 2001, Johnston's AMWU (Australian Manufacturing Workers Union) mob broke through the front door with a crowbar, smashed computers, tore pictures from the walls, let off fire extinguishers and terrified the staff. With national elections only months away, Labor leader Kim Beazley was deeply embarrassed by this outbreak of union thuggery. But when the law threatened, Shorten went in to bat for Johnston, joining delegations to plead on his behalf to Bracks and the ACTU secretary, Greg Combet. They were ignored. At an ACTU event in June, Shorten manoeuvred Johnston and a group of "new militants" into a photograph with Beazley. He and Combet were furious, fearing the photograph would be used as a bargaining chip to compel their support for Johnston, who was charged, a couple of days later, with riot, affray, criminal damage and aggravated burglary. At this, Shorten backed off, apologised to Beazley and lent his support to calls for a new code of conduct on picket lines. He declared: "We recognise unions need to be strong and militant at times and vigorous on picket lines but not violent and not unlawful." The *Age* mocked the idea of a code. What might it say? "How about simply: 'Keep the peace?'"

Sword, determined to block what seemed Shorten's inevitable rise to the state presidency in June 2002, pulled off a daring faction play. He took the NUW out of Labor Unity and into a pact with the Socialist Left. Driven by little more than Sword's hatred of the ShortCons, this "modernisation alliance" gave the Left mastery over the Victorian party for the first time in a decade. Vengeance was in the air: Feeney was sacked as state secretary; Marles lost preselection for the seat of Corio; and Shorten lost the race for the state presidency. For the first and one of the last times in his rise to power, Bill Shorten hit a wall. His rivals derided him as "Bye Bye Bill." A union insider calling himself Delia Delegate observed in *Crikey*: "His flag is barely still flying, riddled with bullet-holes and mud and blood. His friends say he regrets ever running for President, suspecting that his over-reaching may have triggered the whole split of the Right."

In Canberra, which for Victorian purposes might be called the outside world, Beazley had been toppled after his crushing defeat in the *Tampa* election. Simon Crean failed to inspire excitement as leader of the Opposition. In December 2003, Shorten backed the transition to Mark Latham. His support inspired no affection in the new man. "When I first became leader, Ludwig and Little Billy Shorten pledged AWU support for me," Latham wrote in his diary six months later. "But you can't trust them as far as you can kick them." Nevertheless, Latham was guest of honour at the 2004 annual AWU shindig at Crown Casino and sat on Shorten's left. Latham was surprised to find the union leader urging him to support the free trade agreement being negotiated by the Howard government:

I said that I thought both he and his union were against it, to which he responded, "That's just for the members. We need to say that sort of thing when they reckon their jobs are under threat. I want it to go through. The US Alliance is too important to do otherwise. Politically, you have no choice." Great, the two faces of Little Billy Shorten: Public Shorten against the FTA, Private Billy in favour of it. Is this why he's being groomed for one of the top slots in the corporation? Political courage is not his long suit. Not a bad night otherwise.

Shorten stood above the ruck. Most weeks found him giving speeches. He was writing opinion pieces calling for the defence of jobs, an educated workforce and protection from the pain of globalisation: "The key challenge of future policy will be to manage change with equity." The triumph of his Press Club debut was a couple of years behind him. How journalists had salivated when they found Richard Pratt, ACI Glass Packaging's Peter Robinson, Smorgon's industrial manager Andrew Ashbridge and a squad of Labor leaders gathered in Canberra to watch the young AWU boss do his stuff that day. His theme was the humanising record of unions in the history of Australia: "Yet the Howard Government sells us as the enemy at the gates." The AWU had polled its own members and he knew the men and women of the union overwhelmingly supported Howard blocking the *Tampa*. That election proved a life lesson for Shorten: he saw the power of wedge politics. At the Press Club a few months later, he called on unions to act as a conservative check on the rank and file. Unions represent 2 million workers and who, he asked, do Labor's branches represent?

> There is a problem in the party structures when my wife's football club, Hawthorn, has more members than the ALP in Victoria. Some branches are dominated by the few who can endure the *Survivor*-like test of monthly attendances at suburban branch meetings.
>
> Often, it is the union votes at a state conference that stop extremist ALP branch rank-and-file resolutions from becoming party policy. Unions have proven to be useful at assisting the process of sensible party management. If we were to remove union involvement from preselections, there is no guarantee that small inner-suburban ALP branches will get it right.

After Labor's next beating in October 2004, Shorten published a hard critique of Latham's policies and campaign. It was a bold move. By this time, he had been elected to the party's national executive. Even so, he had no official imprimatur to launch this attack. From one defeat to the next, his message had not changed:

Labor's task now is to move to the centre ...

Howard has retained his conservative supporters in the Right intelligentsia, while gaining newer
supporters in "Middle Australia" through his
"dog-whistle" rhetoric about issues such as border security, gay marriage and the US alliance.

By contrast, Labor's support has been increas-
ingly confined to the Left intelligentsia with its
post-Whitlam emphasis on progressive policies on
the environment, refugees and multiculturalism.
The policy priorities of the Left are not wrong,
but they have acquired a prominence that is now a
barrier to Labor reconnecting with both its blue-
collar base and middle Australia. The issues of
greatest concern to the Left must become less
prominent in Labor campaigning.

Howard understands the power of wedge
politics ...

Labor should reject the suggestion that any
connection to trade unions is an electoral liability.
The everyday experience of working for the eco-
nomic interests of people in the real economy is a
valuable policy anchor ...

Latham dismissed this in his diary as "absolute
horseshit." A few weeks later, in January 2005,
Latham was gone and Shorten took a leading role in

restoring Beazley to the party leadership. Kevin Rudd had rushed home from the tsunami-devastated coasts of Asia to find his way to the top blocked by an alliance of the Right factions in Queensland, New South Wales and Victoria. They hadn't been as united in a decade. Rudd was persuaded to keep out of the way and allowed the old leader to return with maximum grace.

Victoria was again in turmoil, but this time Shorten was riding triumphantly above the confusion. He had pulled off the greatest factional coup of his career. It had taken time, patience and perseverance, but the impact on Labor would be profound. First, Sword fell. The old leader had made the mistake of surrounding himself with young people of talent and ambition while maintaining an iron grip on the union. His protégés came for him in early 2004. Over lunch in a North Melbourne bistro they told Sword his was "a magnificent achievement," but it was time to go. He did so with great dignity. The man who took his place as Victorian secretary of the NUW was an old Young Labor sparring partner of Shorten's, Martin Pakula. Public assurances were given that the NUW's "modernisation alliance" with the Left was there to stay. But Shorten and the hirsute Pakula began to talk. They talked all year. In late November, Pakula brought the NUW back into Labor Unity. They called the new alliance Renewal. The deal was done in writing: a peace treaty between warring unions that restored the old order in Victorian Labor and handed power to the ShortCons. For these faction warriors, this was a career-defining achievement. "The resulting alliance now controls about 56 per cent of the numbers in the state branch," Michael Bachelard wrote in the *Australian*. "But such deals come with a price, and their currency is seats in parliament."

The state conference in May 2005 was as vitriolic as anyone could remember, as the Left confronted the reality of Shorten's pact with Pakula. It was a Christmas tree of preselection deals all the way down to little local councils on the fringes of Melbourne. Six members of federal parliament – three of them Opposition frontbenchers – were to be ousted simultaneously. Shorten was promised Maribyrnong. The scale of the operation and the factional conflict it generated through 2005 had not been seen in Victoria for a generation. In August, Shorten further consolidated his position by persuading hardliner Dean Mighell to take the Electrical Trades Union out of the Socialist Left and deliver him another handful of votes. The two men had dealt with each other before as supporters of the run-through rabble-rouser Craig Johnston. The price demanded by Mighell? One federal seat and two in the Victorian parliament.

"I do think the Labor Party needs to constantly be regenerating its parliamentary bloodline," Shorten told Network Ten's *Meet the Press*. That's undisputed. In the melee that consumed Labor in Victoria for nearly a year, a number of difficult political truths had to be faced. Old parliamentarians don't go easily. They fight. To the defence of their little stretch of leather, they bring all their survival skills. But there has to be turnover. In other parties and other states, change is more orderly. The spoils are divided. But in Labor in Victoria, with its shifting loyalties, the factions on top at any particular moment take all. Winners win big and losers lose big. "There are no worries about broken hearts," says Combet. "You have to be tough to survive and Shorten is tough." Victoria is brutal but a great political school. "It throws up people trained in the art of politics," says Gerry Kitchener, a veteran of Labor politics in the state who became an adviser to Julia Gillard. He is not talking about the development of policy – sadly, that's a separate issue – but drumming in basic skills:

> You cannot get a better grounding anywhere in the world. There's dozens upon dozens of people trained in the mechanics of politics in this state through the factional system. They know what they're doing: they know about polls, they know

how to run campaigns. So you've got this ground-ing. If you want a professional machine, you can't just snap your fingers and expect people to have all these skills.

And the machine is not entirely blind to talent. It can't be. The factions don't guarantee the best people win seats – far from it – but the machine knows talent is survival. Among the time-servers, the burnt-out hacks and the sons of Labor fathers sorted into the parliaments of the nation, there has to be some talent or the party will never see power. As Melbourne was distracted by the Commonwealth Games in early 2006, a new Labor team of promise was selected for Canberra. The Renewal pact took some knocks. Three of the six designated victims managed to sur-vive – the three scalps that had been promised to Pakula and Mighell. What Shorten was promised, he secured. Shorten emerged triumphant.

Isaacs

Anne Corcoran did not go quietly. No one did in these months. She raged against branch stacking. "What is democratic," she asked the *Age*, "about a whole pile of members who don't know they belong to the party, who are having their subscriptions paid for them, who get dragged in by kombi van to a polling booth, given a bit of paper and told, 'You go in there and mark the paper just exactly like this, and we'll take you home again in a few minutes'? How democratic is that?" She won 56 per cent of the local vote. But that was only the first step of the process. In Victoria, equal weight in a Labor preselection is given to the vote of the party's 100-member Public Office Selection Committee. Between them, Shorten and Mighell had sixty or more of those votes. Corcoran was overwhelmed. The contest went to the barrister Mark Dreyfus QC. He was not a faction warrior but a talent pick who became Attorney-General in Rudd's second government and is now Shadow Attorney-General and Shadow Minister for the Arts.

Corio

"I'm not going to have some snot-nosed apparatchik from the right wing of the Labor Party dictating to my constituency who they will have as member," declared Gavan O'Connor. He was wrong. Richard Marles beat him soundly in the local ballot. In the last stages of the contest, an ex-girlfriend of Marles accused him, Feeney, Andrew Landeryou and an unnamed fourth "amigo" of running a slush fund to pay party memberships in Corio. She swore in a statutory declaration: "Richard Marles explained to me that these people would never join if they had to pay their own fees so it was important that enough money was raised or sourced by him during the year to pay for these fees or else he would lose 'numbers.'" All three men denied the allegation. Marles became Minister for Trade in Rudd's second government and is now Shadow Minister for Immigration and Border Protection.

Scullin

Harry Jenkins survived a bizarre challenge from a kid called Nathan Murphy from the Electrical Trades Union. He was a protégé of Mighell with not a single run on the board. Even those who negotiated this deal were reported to be embarrassed. Jenkins of the Socialist Left, who had held this rock-solid Labor seat for nearly twenty years, won 62 per cent of the local vote. Shorten's forces were unable to override the rank-and-file mandate. Jenkins was Speaker under Rudd and Gillard, and retired at the 2013 election.

Bruce

Alan Griffin also survived. He was once considered a Labor star for having defeated Shorten's father-in-law, Julian Beale, in 1996, when the rest of the nation was voting the other way. A decade later he was considered ripe for plucking. But he won the local vote handsomely and survived before the selection committee because of the defection of one unknown right-wing delegate. Griffin had the portfolio of veterans affairs under Rudd, to which was added the portfolio of defence personnel under Gillard.

Hotham

The challenge to Simon Crean shocked Labor. He had been leader of the Opposition a little more than a year earlier. It was too soon. Gillard stood up for him. Beazley's refusal to intervene on behalf of his old adversary lost him friends in caucus. Crean effortlessly outsmarted Martin Pakula on the ground, winning an overwhelming 70 per cent of the local vote. The selection committee rubber-stamped the local verdict. Crean became a hero of the party rank and file across the nation. The win revived his fortunes. He became Minister for Trade under Rudd and Minister for Regional Australia, Regional Development and Local Government under Gillard.

But Pakula was NUW and had to be looked after. He was bright and ambitious, with economics and law degrees under his belt. As a consolation prize, the party gave him a seat in the Victorian upper house. That left an unhappy Sang Nguyen, to whom Labor Unity had promised the upper house seat in return for mustering votes in the Vietnamese community. "I've done everything they requested and made no mistakes," he told Michael Bachelard of the *Australian*. "Martin lost his preselection in Hotham, that is his fault, not my fault. Now I have to pay the price." He was particularly furious with Shorten, having, he said, done so much to secure the man's preselection. "There are 70 Vietnamese members in Maribyrnong. I campaigned hard for him. I went doorknocking with him, went to Vietnamese houses with him." Labor's national executive confirmed the discarding of Nguyen. Pakula is now Attorney-General of Victoria.

Maribyrnong
At the seventh annual AWU ball at Crown Casino in October 2005, Bob Hawke led the 1200-strong crowd in all four verses of the old union anthem "Solidarity Forever":

> Is there aught we hold in common with the greedy
> parasite,
> Who would lash us into serfdom and would crush
> us with his might?
> Is there anything left to us but to organise and
> fight?
> For the union makes us strong.

The great of the party had been gathered by Shorten to endorse his push on Canberra. Beazley declared it a

privilege to share the platform with "one of our thinkers" and "a terrific union leader in the Bob Hawke
tradition." Conroy, Wayne Swan, Craig Emerson and
old Bill Ludwig were there. Absent were Kevin Rudd
and the sitting member for Maribyrnong, Bob Sercombe. He told the papers he was still waiting for his
invitation.

Sercombe had known Shorten was after him for
years and had done all he could to shore up his position in this solid Labor stretch of Melbourne that
runs south and west of Tullamarine and Essendon
airports. For half a dozen years Shorten had been a
busy presence in one of the branches in Moonee
Ponds. Shorten saw this as doing the chores of a keen
member of the party. Sercombe reckoned he was on
the prowl. It was a strategic mistake by the old man
to abandon the ShortCons in 2002 and go with
Sword's Modernisation Alliance. Yet it won him
friends at the time. Crikey reported that Sword's
backers, who hitherto thought Sercombe "a branch-
stacking oaf," now called him "a magnificent builder
of relationships with ethnic communities, encouraging them to participate in the democratic process."
But when Sword fell, Sercombe was left exposed in
the selection committee, though regarded as almost
unbeatable on the ground. He had increased Labor's
lead over the Liberals to nearly 10,000 at the 2004

election. Maribyrnong was known in the party as "Fortress Bob."

But in late 2005, Shorten came to terms with one of the dark legends of the Victorian party, George Seitz, who had been stacking in Maribyrnong for twenty years. No scandal had ever budged Seitz. His energy was endless and so was the money he had on hand to pay party memberships. The Serbian-born Seitz was both state member for Keilor and a power in the Brimbank City Council. Both lay across the map of Maribyrnong. His elite troops were the mainly Macedonian members of the local Sydenham Park Soccer Club, which carries on its clubhouse wall the mission statement "To continually promote all that is righteous in the name of football." Seitz would claim on his deathbed in 2015 that he was persuaded to switch allegiance from Sercombe to Shorten because of the young man's great prospects: "He is the next prime minister, or I hope. That is the basis upon which I supported him." Shorten also tied up Vietnamese votes through Sang Nguyen and Turkish votes through Seitz's detested local rival Hakki Suleyman. The Shorten campaign in Maribyrnong would be all the more colourful for the street brawls that broke out between the Seitz and Suleyman forces. But both were working for him. It was yet another of the unlikely alliances which have advanced his career.

Before the formalities of the preselection were complete, he was able to save Seitz from forced retirement. He was sixty-four and the premier had decreed that all Labor MPs in the state must retire at sixty-five. Shorten chaired a meeting of the administrative committee of the party in early 2006 that exempted Seitz from Bracks' decree. Seitz would go on stacking branches until his retirement in 2010.

Sercombe did not go gently. Offers were made and refused. Shorten was polite. He acknowledged the man's long service but argued it was time for change: "We haven't won a federal election since 1993. When your footy team loses four consecutive grand finals, you renew the team." Less elegant were the efforts of his old mate Andrew Landeryou, who pummelled Sercombe week after week in his scandal blog *The Other Cheek*:

> The OC notes that Carmen Sercombe is in fact a very pleasant person, in contrast to the stream of shonks, two-bit crooks, Chinese deal-makers, spooks, sleaze-balls, muck-rakers, branch-stackers, fixers, and scumbags populating the office of Bob Sercombe. I don't know anyone in the ALP who has an unkind word to say about her. But don't start them on Bob.

Landeryou was correspondingly kind to Shorten:
"Sercs made an important contribution once, now his
sole role in life is blocking a future leader of the ALP
from getting preselected. It's a sad way for it all to end."

Shorten knocked on hundreds of doors. He coyly
brushed off talk of his ambition. To the people of
Sunshine and Essendon, Moonee Ponds and St
Albans, he sent a letter of commendation from a
remarkable tag team of backers: not only Beazley,
Bracks, Hawke, Premier of Queensland Peter Beattie,
Bill Ludwig, the New South Wales Right's Mark
Arbib and ACTU president Sharan Burrow, but also
his old school friend and executive director of the
conservative Institute of Public Affairs, John Roskam,
and one of the nation's most successful businessmen.
"He's hard-working," said Richard Pratt. "He has
vision, he's a good communicator and he is interested
in the wellbeing of people."

After all that, he won only a narrow victory in the
streets of Maribyrnong. Sercombe, with nearly half
the local vote, did not see himself as out of the preselection race. He believed his friend Mighell would use
his votes on the selection committee to save him.
"The old saying about a trade unionist's handshake
being his bond applies, especially as Dean says he is
about traditional Labor values," said Sercombe. But
he was talking about another party at another time.

Mighell had done a deal with Shorten. When it was clear he had been deserted, Sercombe withdrew from the race and didn't hold back. He told ABC Radio: "The central problem in the Victorian branch over recent years is they've got an extremely arrogant, very feral Right seeking to throw their muscle round and take everything in their wake." He lashed Shorten: "He's not the messiah, he's just a naughty right-wing boy."

Love Me Do: 11 June 2015

The old Female Orphan School on the campus of the University of Western Sydney is a shrine to Gough and Margaret Whitlam. There's a gallery upstairs named after her and the shop stocks "It's Time" t-shirts. Gathered downstairs in a room that may once have been a dormitory for desperate children are forty university students come to listen to the leader of the Opposition. "What I'm interested in doing is engaging," he tells them. "By engaging, I mean listening. I want to hear your point of view." There are television cameras in the room and a posse of journalists. Breaking all round him that week is news of the deals he had done with Cleanevent and Winslow Constructions all those years ago at the AWU. This would be addressed in a news conference in the courtyard afterwards. With the students he's talking university fees, computer coding, the republic and the damage done to him by so many years of plane travel: "Doctors say I have flight attendant ears."

It's a curious performance: chatty and partisan. He's beating up on the Abbott government and laying on the charm. It's odd to watch the man who would be prime minister trying so hard to be their pal. He takes questions three or four at a time. It's a new technique to let politicians riff freely across half a dozen topics without answering anything in particular. He's not entirely evasive. He's blunt about refugees. Once or twice he earns points by admitting he hasn't an answer: "That's a work in progress." It's hard to gauge the students' mood but they seem pleased to be in Shorten's presence – not remotely awed, but pleased. He is easier to read. He stands before them with his hands in his pockets and a look on his face that says: love me.

So much has been written about this man since he became chief of the AWU fifteen years ago. That's when the newspaper profiles began. There is, for such a brief career, a hefty pile of them. Every profile addresses Shorten's profound self-belief. Every interview about his childhood and university years turns up fresh evidence of his precocious determination to be prime minster. His confidence in himself only grew with time. It irks his colleagues. "He's a capable guy," John Button once remarked on ABC Radio. "In fact, he's mentioned that to me himself several times." His will to power makes sense of his career.

As a former Gillard minister told me: "He wants to be PM because he wants to be PM. Everything is about him becoming PM." That takes more than self-belief. Shorten is a serious candidate because he is also willing to lead the life it takes to reach the top: a life hostage at every point to public scrutiny, luck and the intrigue of his colleagues.

But there's a subplot here: his hunger for public affection. Margaret Simons spotted it early in a fine profile written a decade ago as Shorten was manoeuvring to win Maribyrnong:

> Bill Shorten likes to be liked, and he is good at it too. He is handsome, smart, boyishly charming and a reflex flatterer. He is almost a flirt. His weakness, say those who know him, is that he needs to bask in the glow of others' love and admiration. He needs to be loved.

Most politicians do. It's magazine Freud: turning to the public to fill the void. Shorten works at love. He is good with people. He has to an astonishing degree a politician's knack for remembering names and the stories of strangers' lives. He connects. His best work is done face to face. Men and women senior in the party talk of him making contact years ago when they were no more than budding talents. He began bringing them in even then, building his base, recruiting. But in the rough and tumble of the party, his pursuit of affection can seem a little desperate. "It really drives him nuts when someone doesn't like him," a leading adversary in the faction wars told me. "He has to be loved. Even when he fucks you over he wants you to like him – he rings and tries to make up."

Shorten doesn't thrive on hostility. It's hard to imagine him staring down the unions as Hawke did to open the Australian economy to the world. It's hard to see him trying to persuade Australia to change its mind on any great issue. He works with what's there. By temperament and political disposition he is a numbers man. Shorten isn't built to stand up to panic in the name of principle. A fundamental political lesson of his career was the great wedge of 2001, when Howard took Australia with him by stopping the *Tampa*. Beazley had briefly allowed himself to be wedged. Shorten is determined to avoid that fate. It isn't true he stands for nothing. There's a list of decent, Labor policies he's always backed: jobs, prosperity, education and health. What's counted against him is that he stands for nothing brave.

A student asks: what will Labor do about plans to strip Australians of their citizenship? Shorten won't pledge to block them. He promises merely to be "consistent and constructive." He boasts of Labor's fine-tuning of Abbott's many security laws: "We have made plenty of changes and the government has accepted them." He's asked about refugees and his answer includes the detail that "Richard Pratt was a four-year-old refugee who fled Poland." Would they have a clue who that was? Could they work out where Shorten stands in all this? He's so fuzzy. With great charm he thanks them for their "outstanding questions and a couple of policy suggestions" and departs with the cameras, the press and the acting vice-chancellor in tow.

Apprentice: 2006 to 2010

B y the time the Beaconsfield mine disaster was done and dusted, the papers were baying for Shorten to move straight to the Lodge. A few days after Brant Webb and Todd Russell were pulled alive from their rock tomb, Sydney's *Daily Telegraph* splashed across page one: "Bill for PM. Odds Shorten on next Labor leader." Talking for a fortnight at a pithead in northern Tasmania turned Shorten into a national figure. He'd flown home when there seemed no hope of survivors, but when two men were discovered to be alive down there he borrowed Richard Pratt's jet to fly back – just in time, his detractors said, for the Seven Network's *Sunrise*. The town was a mess of miners, press crews and rescue teams. Everything he had learnt at Longford he applied in spades at Beaconsfield. The miners told him what was going on below ground and he told the press. They were hungry for stories. He fed them. There were quotable quotes: drilling through Beaconsfield quartz was like "throwing a Kleenex at rock." Richard Carleton of *60 Minutes* asked the mine manager the tough question: why was it, after an earlier rock fall at the spot where the miners were trapped, "that you continue to send men in to work in such a dangerous environment?" He was then felled on the spot by a heart attack. Shorten wasn't asking any tough questions. He promised those later. "We cannot afford," he said, "to distract from the issue of rescuing the men." Bob Ellis rhapsodised:

> He gave, too, and everybody noticed it, new credibility to the union movement and he did it knowingly. He played the matchless boon of those nine days of media attention like a trusty old harmonica and turned round the popular view of unions as gangs of rorting thugs to decent, conscienceful guardians of Middle Australia, and their safety and their work conditions ... He had clarity, dander, humour, class feeling, momentum, a massive IQ and scads of ambition. He was like Bob Hawke in, say, 1978: on a roll.

But there would be no sudden assumption to Canberra. In May 2006, a fortnight after Beaconsfield, an ACNielsen poll took the wind out of his sails: a mere 9 per cent of those surveyed thought him the best person to lead the country. He came in a distant fourth behind Julia Gillard with 28 per cent, Kevin Rudd with 26 per cent and the struggling Kim Beazley with 21 per cent. And in any case, Bob Sercombe was determined to remain the member for Maribyrnong as long as he possibly could. He invited anyone gullible enough to think he might resign early "to ring me so I can sell them the Sydney Harbour Bridge."

Shorten cleared the decks a little. He handed Cesar Melhem the state secretary's post but remained national boss of the AWU and as busy a factional player as ever in the party. There were still deals to be done. In December, he joined the union bosses who failed to save Beazley in the showdown that brought Kevin Rudd to the leadership. Twice now, Shorten had voted against Rudd. He and the new man would not be natural allies.

Shorten threw himself into the coming election campaign as if every dollar counted. "Maribyrnong was what people would call a safe seat," he told the royal commission. "But I was a new candidate and I was committed to my constituents in Maribyrnong, to make sure that I took the campaign seriously." As AWU boss he had dispensed money to election candidates for years: a few hundred dollars here, a few thousand there. Now the money was flowing to him. The Pratts' mansion, Raheen, was the setting for extravagantly successful fundraisers. The union was backing Shorten's campaign. "The AWU was on full campaign mode across Australia," he told the royal commission. "We wanted to defeat John Howard and get rid of his WorkChoices laws." And Shorten was turning to the political and business world for the cash he needed to take him to Canberra.

Brian Burke had seen tough times since he turned up to Shorten's Young Labor shindigs in Melbourne. Reports appeared early in the Maribyrnong campaign that the ex-jailbird and former Labor premier of Western Australia had "re-emerged as an influential player and advises Mr Shorten behind the scenes." In fact, they had been working together for years. Shorten loved Burke. Sometime in the decade after the once-popular politician emerged from prison, Shorten employed him to make peace with union rivals in Western Australia. "Unions can waste a lot of time on demarcation disputes," Shorten explained. "Burke helped us build a relationship with the CFMEU and Kevin Reynolds." Later, Burke helped beat off a challenge to the local AWU leadership. He was riding high again and his lobbying business was flourishing. He held big fundraising bashes for Labor politicians at Perugino restaurant in Perth, including one for Rudd and another for Shorten. But in late 2006, Burke became a pariah once again when the Corruption and Crime

Commission of Western Australia revealed him establishing a covert channel of communication to a minister in the state government. John Howard pounced on Labor's links to Burke. Rudd was fearfully embarrassed. Shorten almost escaped unscathed until Laura Tingle of the *Financial Review* heard a whisper about the Shorten fundraiser. She rang the ALP head office. Seven hours later, Shorten rang to say he had paid the $20,000 back. Next day Tingle reported: "Mr Shorten said he had realised only late last week that cheques had come in to his office, and he had told the ALP's national office yesterday of the funds raised."

In late 2006, Shorten asked Ted Lockyer of Unibuilt, "Ted, would you be willing to employ someone to support my campaign for parliament?" Lockyer was "a bit of a larger-than-life character" who had been dealing with the AWU for a decade or more. He said he was good for $50,000. Shorten had in mind for the job a Young Labor apparatchik called Lance Wilson, who seemed "a good cut of a fellow, young and new." He took Lockyer to a coffee shop round the corner from the union's headquarters in North Melbourne to meet Unibuilt's new employee. Wilson set up a campaign office for the contender in Moonee Ponds and the Unibuilt money began to flow in February 2007.

Several aspects of this arrangement intrigued the royal commission. Sometime before polling day, the union and Unibuilt, a labour hire firm, had to negotiate a fresh EBA. Shorten insisted the gift to his campaign didn't hurt the prospects of his members. Unibuilt expected no favours in return:

> The idea that somehow having a discussion with an employer on two different topics, even if not at the same time, and somehow that it is untoward to raise money for election campaigns and do anything else, to me … that assumes that whenever there is a donation in our electoral system, by anyone, that all other relationships and transactions must immediately be cast into doubt. That is not right, and that is not how I operated at the union.

The paperwork issued by the union falsely stated that Wilson was to be employed by Unibuilt as a researcher. Quite wrong, agreed Shorten: "He was a campaign resource, a campaign director for me." He had asked for the paperwork to be drafted but he can't remember having read it. Again and again, he told Jeremy Stoljar that he left details to his underlings: "When you're the candidate, you don't do all of the paperwork. Your job is to talk to people, be out there."

The deal began to collapse. When the labour hire company proved slow to pay, Wilson was transferred to the AWU payroll and Unibuilt was invoiced $6000 a month. The invoices were also false: they had Wilson working for the AWU rather than Shorten. So how, asked Stoljar, could an auditor tell what the payments were actually for? "You will have to ask the auditor," replied Shorten. And how could the members of the AWU tell from the records? "At the National Executive of the Union there were frequent discussions about how to deal with the WorkChoices laws and the importance of political action against the existing WorkChoices laws."

Unibuilt was about to go bust. After giving a little over $40,000, the payments stopped altogether. From there till polling day, the AWU itself met Wilson's wage. But these gifts from the union and the company were not declared to the Australian Electoral Commission – or not until a few days before Shorten's interrogation before the royal commission in 2015. Why? Shorten said he had only in the last few months discovered the omission. But why wait to amend the declaration until he knew the issue would be raised at the commission? It had taken him and his lawyers till the last minute to find the information, replied Shorten. Politicians of all parties are often guilty of the same failure, he explained. "I can just again say to you:

this should have been completely disclosed at the time. I take ultimate responsibility for that."

Shorten's campaign launch in Sunshine featured the Beaconsfield survivors, Russell and Webb, comedian Max Gillies dressed as John Howard, and the Choir of Hard Knocks singing "Love Is in the Air". Shorten was no ordinary candidate. He hit the road from remote Queensland to western Sydney, attacking WorkChoices and selling Labor's policies for jobs, decent hours and fair treatment at work. By this time, the ACTU chief, Greg Combet, had also opted for Canberra, and Howard was on the hustings painting a terrible picture of union domination should Labor be elected. But the public didn't buy it: an *Age/* Nielsen poll shortly before election day, 2007, showed that only a third of those surveyed believed trade unions would "run the country" under Kevin Rudd. Shorten's argument is that union organisers bring more to parliament than Liberal Party apparatchiks. It's an old theme he buffed for his maiden speech:

> On the boards of a woolshed, you know that shearers earn their pay. When you talk to steelworkers at the Port Kembla blast furnaces, to the underground miners at Mount Isa, to the oil workers in Bass Strait in winter or to those who staff the undertakers' night vans as they deal with

the grief and tragedy of a road trauma or worse, you know you are in the presence of greatness. When you come face to face with heroism, cooperation and fighting spirit in workplace tragedies such as the Longford gas explosion in Victoria or the Beaconsfield mine collapse in Tasmania, you know you are in the presence of ordinary people performing extraordinary deeds. Every company, every work site I have visited for the last 15 years, taught me the potential for greatness that individuals carry within them and showed me the limitless capacity of Australian workers and Australian businesses – and, thus, the limitless potential of the Australian economy and Australian society.

Shorten was as safe as houses in Maribyrnong but the post-Beaconsfield euphoria had long evaporated. There was no suggestion now that he would be catapulted to the highest levels of government. Under the old rules he might have muscled his way into cabinet but Rudd had declared that he, not caucus, would decide the ministry. "I will be leading this show," he told the *7.30 Report*. "When it comes to the outcomes I want, I will get them." He made Shorten parliamentary secretary for disability services. Shorten had known the old guard would be waiting for him with cricket bats in Canberra, but this was humiliating. A few days earlier he had had a staff of a dozen to run a union 100,000-strong. Now he had five men and women in a distant wing of parliament to pursue the unlikely cause of disability reform. The joke around the building was: "We've fixed Bill up with a job as parliamentary secretary for people who can't wipe their own arses."

He sought advice. Gillard told him it was a chance to show another side of himself. Kelty advised him to put his head down and work. "If you want to be really good, you've got to do an apprenticeship in life. Hawke did that. Howard in his miserable way did it too. So did Keating as treasurer. He worked and worked. You've got to work for this job." He meant the leadership. After an angry few days, Shorten decided the only option was success. "This is going to be a campaign," he promised Kelty. "I will not join the queue of do-gooders."

Labor MPs were puzzled to find that the man whose arrival had been heralded by trumpets took so little part in caucus. He rarely put up his hand. "He just didn't trouble the scorers," said one senior Labor figure. Shorten remained a factional warlord and was highly successful in his portfolios, but was not a party leader. "If you looked objectively at who was doing what on the floor of the parliament, who was doing what in policy reform, contributing in the cabinet, contributing in the caucus, contributing in the ministry, it wasn't Shorten. Not even close. Not even in the top tier. Not even part of the A-team." A measure of his absence from the inner workings of power in Canberra can be gauged from the many memoirs already published from this time. Save for his role in the great executions, Shorten's name barely appears in the indexes. He had a lot to learn. Parliament was something entirely new. He told the *Sunday Age* he was warned it would be hard. "People give you this advice from outside of Parliament, and they say, 'Oh, it's like going to the big school now.' And I thought, 'Oh, yeah, I've been around, done a bit.' But they're right. It is big … I'm amazed at what I didn't know about Parliament until I got there."

*

A month after he walked the Kokoda Track in July 2008, Shorten left his wife. To the end, they were regarded as a power couple. They had no children. IVF had failed. Their big house in Moonee Ponds was empty. Shorten told an old comrade from Young Labor: "It's nothing to do with my sperm." In the last months before coming to Canberra, he had met the daughter of the governor of Queensland. The *Courier-Mail*'s vice-regal column noted in September 2007: "In

the evening, the Governor received the call of Ms
Chloe Bryce-Parkin and Mr Bill Shorten." No one
was reading the tea-leaves. Chloe was formidably
glamorous, wife of the resort architect Roger Parkin, a
mother of two and spokeswoman for Cement Australia. The Shortens parted in August 2008. It is always
reported that he left his first wife abruptly at a football
game. "That's plain wrong," says Shorten. Many doors
in Establishment Melbourne shut in his face. Others
opened, for in September his new partner's mother
became governor-general. Chloe was pregnant in the
winter of 2009 and they married in Melbourne that
November: she in white, he in a grey pinstripe suit
with a rose in his lapel. This time the ceremony was at
St Thomas Anglican Church in Moonee Ponds. To the
utter bafflement of his friends, Shorten had become an
Anglican.

"I believe in God," he says. "Like a lot of Australians I don't want to talk about my faith, but I'm not
an atheist. I think that things happen with the influence of God. My wife wanted us to be married in the
Anglican faith and there was a very good priest who
supported us. So I thought, fair enough, I'm happy to
belong to a church willing to marry two people who
are divorced." He hasn't reneged on Catholicism
entirely. Pope Francis he thinks impressive: "A
remarkable guy. A breath of fresh air." Catholic

social teaching is still in his head, along with the "golden rule" every boy was taught at Xavier: "It was at the heart of the Jesuit call to be a 'man for others.' And I have spent my working life, both representing workers and as parliamentarian, trying to measure up to this standard of compassion and empathy." What repels Shorten are "Sunday Christians who wear their religiosity on their sleeves and then lecture people all week. I'm uncomfortable with the view that God has a really strong opinion about who I'm living with. I don't believe that God has a strong view on IVF or stem-cell research." Here he finds Melbourne's relaxed brand of Anglicanism particularly attractive, with its respect for science, acceptance of women priests and attitude to marriage, including same-sex marriage. With a candour not shown by Rudd or Gillard when they were Labor leaders, Shorten called the Australian Christian Lobby on its vengeful attitudes to sex and marriage. This is personal for him:

> When I hear people invoking the scriptures to attack blended families like mine, I cannot stay silent. I do not agree. When I see people hiding behind the Bible to insult and demonise people based on who they love, I cannot stay silent. I do not agree. When I hear people allege that "God tells them" that marriage equality is the first step

on the road to polygamy and bigamy and bestiality, I cannot stay silent. I do not agree. These prejudices do not reflect the Christian values I believe in ... I believe in God and I believe in marriage equality under the civil law of the Commonwealth of Australia.

*

War had broken out again in Victoria. Hostilities began with the ShortCons trying to pay their debts to the Turkish stackers in Maribyrnong. They were owed the preselection of Natalie Suleyman for the state seat of Kororoit. When this was blocked by rival George Seitz, the Right began to tear itself apart. Things came to a head after six months with an attempt to knock off the state secretary of the party, Stephen Newnham. Premier John Brumby put his own job on the line to beat back the challenge. A few weeks later, Shorten regained his grip on the party with a daring manoeuvre: he took the Short-Cons out of Labor Unity and into a pact with former teacher Kim Carr, the lion of the Socialist Left. Together they could carve up the seats between them. Feeney was betrayed and Labor Unity reduced to a rump. Once again, a splendid name was found for this pragmatic bastardry: the Stability Pact. "It is a bit tough," remarked one of the now powerless faction leaders, "to describe Pearl Harbor as a stability agreement." For six months the pact was assailed by the far Right and far Left, until a fresh peace was struck between Shorten and Feeney in June 2009. Stability Pact II delivered yet more votes to Shorten in the councils of the party in Victoria. Along the way, a successor was found for Newnham. The deal was done by telephone hook-up out of the deputy prime minister's office. Gillard's adviser Gerry Kitchener recalls: "Parliament was sitting – it turns out that the next day Conroy was introducing the NBN legislation – and there's Gillard, Feeney, Conroy, Shorten on the phone with Brumby and a couple of his advisors in Gillard's office, locked away for three hours thrashing out a deal on who became State Secretary. It was the ultimate obsession about the factional stuff."

Shorten had taken up the cause of the disabled with passion. Gillard wrote: "He actually fell in love with the policy area and the possibility of making change for so many Australians leading such difficult lives." Care for the disabled in Australia was a long-recognised shambles. Your fate depended not on need, but on how and where you came by your disability. At birth? On a building site? Insured or uninsured? New South Wales or Queensland? Billions were being spent on care but billions more were needed to do the job properly. Out of Rudd's talk-fest, the Australia 2020 Summit, came the idea of a national insurance scheme rather like Medicare, with every citizen paying a small levy to meet the costs of disability. This idea was not new but had found an effective advocate in Bruce Bonyhady, a banker who had two sons with cerebral palsy. Shorten knew nothing about disability care. Bonyhady taught him. A few weeks after the summit, Shorten appointed a team of bankers and financiers to investigate the insurance scheme. The hope was that they would find fresh ways of raising the enormous amounts of money required. They had over a year to report, while Shorten brought his AWU experience to the task of welding the disability community into one forceful lobby. He would say: "I wished the sector was as well organised as a trade union." Each group dealing with autism or cerebral palsy or dyslexia railed at governments to meet their individual needs. "That is what has failed spectacularly for decades," Shorten told Laura Tingle. "So what you've got to do is give them a common set of claims." He called what he was doing "a case of classic old-fashioned organising."

Rudd was full of praise for his efforts. After the brutal fires in the hinterland of Melbourne in early 2009, he added bushfire reconstruction to Shorten's responsibilities. But he did not promote him in the reshuffle of June 2009. Combet went into the cabinet ahead of him and so did the NSW Right boss, Mark Arbib. Commentators took it to be a deliberate snub. A few days later, a disconsolate Shorten called on the US consul-general, Mark Thurston, in Melbourne. Thurston sent a note of their meeting to Washington:

> Shorten makes no bones about his ambitions in federal politics. During a June 11 meeting, Shorten told Consul General that "he did not take this job to stand still." He explained that he had been overlooked for promotion in Prime Minister Rudd's June 6 cabinet reshuffle in order to keep the geographical balance in the cabinet between Victoria and New South Wales. (Comment: Despite words to the contrary, Shorten appeared disappointed while he was discussing this topic. End comment.) ...
>
> Shorten said that he is deeply influenced by Martin Luther King Jr. and quoted from several of his speeches in our meeting with him. While National Secretary of the powerful Australian Workers' Union, he spent time in the United States collaborating with the United Steel Workers' union ... He is widely known for his pro-U.S. stance ...

Bill Shorten is part of a new generation of articulate, young labour union leaders ... He has an MBA from Melbourne University, was close to the late packaging mogul Richard Pratt, and said that in comparison to other union leaders, he is willing to listen to business concerns ...

Shorten, who is somewhat rumpled in appearance, prefers to get down to business quickly in meetings. He is a nimble conversationalist who understands nuance. In addition to being cautious, considered and thoughtful, he is able to skilfully steer away from topics he prefers to avoid ... he admitted that he is still getting his feet wet in Parliament and that things there are "more complicated than he thought." Despite his lukewarm relationship with Prime Minister Rudd (he sided with Kim Beazley in the 2006 ALP leadership ballot), Shorten struck us as highly ambitious but willing to wait – at least for a while – for his moment in the sun.

The Shortens began to appear together as he went about his political chores. Their daughter Clementine was born a few months after their marriage. To Shorten's delight he found himself a father of three: one of his own and two of Chloe's. He told an old friend from his Monash days: "That's what it's all about."

Everything was going well in Canberra. Rudd appointed him to his little committee of Left and Right powerbrokers who were supposed to settle preselection disputes across the country. Even so, Shorten was never part of Rudd's circle. Neither Kevin nor Therese warmed to him. Yet there was no doubt the prime minister backed his work on disability reform. When the bankers and financiers endorsed the National Disability Insurance Scheme, Rudd passed the idea to the Productivity Commission. Shorten declared the cause "the last practical frontier of civil rights."

Then Rudd began to fall apart. By early winter 2010 he was distrusted by caucus and loathed by most of his ministers. Plans to tax the bonanza being enjoyed by mining companies in one of the great booms in Australian history rallied enemies inside and outside the party. Elections were due within months. Published polls suggested Labor had a fight on its hands. Private polling commissioned by the party was pointing to heavy losses. In Maribyrnong and on the disability circuit Shorten was listening to voters disgruntled and bemused by the direction Rudd was taking. By June he had formed the view that the government was "in electoral trouble of a very serious nature." He was coming to the conclusion: "We had to do something significant." On the

Queen's Birthday weekend he was with Rudd in Western Australia, helping sell the mining tax to miners. Barrie Cassidy reports in *The Party Thieves* that Shorten decided to break with Rudd at a doorstop interview on that trip:

> He was dismayed to hear Rudd talk of how he intended to carve up the infrastructure dividend from the mining tax. Rudd told the media that he would split the money three ways between Western Australia, Queensland and the rest of Australia. Shorten found that a bizarre formula that ran counter to all the principles of federation. He had heard and seen enough. At that moment, he decided that as soon as he returned to the eastern states, he would seek a meeting with Gillard.

A few days later he warned her that Labor might well be wiped out and raised the possibility of her challenging Rudd. He said she "should think about this." Gillard kept her own counsel.

Shorten was not the chief assassin. The idea of sacking the prime minister had been in the air for weeks in Canberra. He was not the first person to urge Gillard to run. The NSW Right minister Tony Burke had raised that with her several times. Unauthorised polling in Victoria was brought to Gillard that showed her approval rating climbing through the roof. The party also polled in four marginal NSW seats, and officials who saw the results on Friday 18 June thought, "We're bloody stuffed." When a by-election next day at the foot of the Blue Mountains saw a 25 per cent swing against Labor, the Right in New South Wales was ready to trigger a caucus spill. On the Monday, the *Australian* carried a most encouraging Newspoll that showed Labor in a winning position, with a two-party-preferred vote of 52 to 48. Rudd was delighted but it didn't give the plotters pause. Shorten wanted Rudd gone but on the night of 22 June he clearly did not know what would happen next. He would say: "It was spontaneous."

A *Sydney Morning Herald* story claiming Rudd was suspicious of Gillard's intentions set the coup in motion. Feeney thought the story the last straw and saw Arbib. Together they went to Gillard's office about 9.30 a.m. She was furious. They urged her to run. The Right of Victoria and New South Wales were already in lock-step, but it was only after this meeting with Gillard that the two faction leaders brought Conroy and Shorten into the loop. From this point, all four men were active players in Rudd's downfall. Arbib was their leader but Kitchener says: "I honestly don't think she would've moved without Shorten." After Question Time, the four met Gillard in Kim Carr's office for over an hour. For connoisseurs of faction play, it was a notable gathering of old enemies and fresh allies brought together in the Stability Pact. But it was not without strain. At some point in this remarkable day, Feeney is said to have told Shorten: "Don't mistake this for unity on the Victorian Right." Gillard went to see Rudd. While that meeting continued, Shorten and a group of plotters went to the Hoang Hau restaurant in Kingston. Cameras followed them. Shorten was filmed making many calls on his mobile phone. He insists he was not rallying the numbers but talking to his step-daughter's teacher. Right or wrong, what the cameras saw that night became what Shorten calls the "infamous footage" of the plot against Rudd.

Gillard was with Rudd for two hours. They came to a strange arrangement: Rudd would step down if, closer to the time, it was felt he was an impediment to Labor's re-election. Senator John Faulkner would act as umpire. Gillard went to an anteroom in the prime minister's suite and rang Conroy. He told her it was too late. Caucus had already made up its mind. She went back to Rudd. "I am now advised that you no longer have the confidence of the caucus," she said. "I am therefore requesting a leadership ballot." She returned to her own office, which soon filled with MPs. They were crunching her numbers.

Kitchener would tell the ABC television series *The Killing Season*:

> Shorten was in the office, he was down the back, but he throughout the evening was bringing MPs – a lot of MPs from Queensland – to meet with Julia. I think it's fair to say that whatever Bill's faults may or may not be, he knows how to work the numbers and he was bringing people until late in the night.

Everyone else had stopped but Shorten kept going. "He was still dragging people in at 1.30 in the morning when Gillard was leaving to go home," says Kitchener. "It was all over Red Rover and he chased down every single vote possible." Later, in the corridors, Kitchener bumped into Arbib, who, never one to miss an opportunity, pulled out a wish-list for Gillard's first ministry. He came to Shorten's name. Kitchener told the ABC:

> He said you couldn't trust Bill Shorten, that he would do Julia in, that the one thing she couldn't do was ever give him industrial relations, because he would use it to solidify the union base to knock her off.

She would do that, and he did that, but Arbib claims Kitchener's account of his warning is rubbish. On the far side of a difficult election campaign in August, which Gillard barely survived, Shorten was called to Yarralumla to be sworn in by his mother-in-law as Assistant Treasurer and Minister for Financial Services and Superannuation. He still had no seat at the cabinet table.

Minister: 2010 to 2013

From this distance, it may seem Gillard's ministers did nothing for three years but plot. Yet a good deal of work was done. Shorten attacked the task of patching up the superannuation system with the energy, if not the passion, he had brought to caring for the disabled. He set about mastering the complications of a system that had produced the fourth biggest pool of retirement funds in the world and an industry that guarded its immense profits with trip-wires and mastiffs. He was embarking on another of the primal battles with money fought by the Rudd and Gillard governments. They lost to miners, Murdoch and poker machines. Shorten pulled off a draw with the superannuation industry.

He worked well with Gillard. They were old factional allies long before the ShortCons forced her hand the night of Rudd's defenestration. Despite the Left label she had worn since her university days, Gillard's career depended on the Right. They gave her Lalor in 1998 on the strength of talent alone.

After that she voted with the Right and they controlled the numbers in her seat. She had her own tiny subfaction known as the Ferguson Left, but her base in Victoria was broad and at its heart were the Short-Cons. She was a party to the Stability Pact. Between the new prime minister and her junior minister for superannuation, there was no factional tension. Nor was he ever a contender for her job. Shorten had spent only three winters in Canberra. Everyone knew his ambitions were huge, but as the Gillard government set to work it seemed that his time, if it were to come, was a long way off. She appointed him to the Expenditure Review Committee. He was not tough. "She wasn't one to bag people, but you knew when she didn't like or respect people," says her adviser Gerry Kitchener. "I think she respected him and I think she respected his talents." But there were ministers who sensed she didn't trust him.

Shorten knew about superannuation. Like many senior union officials, he had been director of an industry fund: in his case, Australian Super, with $30 billion under management. Commercial super funds bleated at times that the new minister had an innate conflict of interest. He stared them down. Shorten fought significant battles on two fronts: one was to compel financial advisers to act in the best interests of their clients, and the other was to provide a standard, simple, low-cost default fund called MySuper, into which everyone's money would be paid unless other arrangements were made. Both ideas had been recommended by several inquiries into the finance industry. Both were fought hard. The behemoth Keating and Hawke had created was more than willing to use its immense resources to oppose change. The independent MP Rob Oakeshott remembers the scene as Shorten began work: "The five peak bodies, pushing competing positions, not only set up camp in the corridors of parliament to give advice, but bombarded electorate offices around Australia with their views."

Shorten's notices were good as he took on the industry in public and private. "This week the apprentice outshone the master," declared the *Australian* in December 2010. "Bill Shorten selling superannuation reforms left Wayne Swan looking second-rate as he struggled to sell his banking measures." What followed was a year's intense advocacy and negotiation. There were complaints that the new minister was not a master of the minutiae as the old minister, Chris Bowen, had been. But Paul Barry, writing on the Power Index website, saw the gap Shorten was filling in Gillard's team:

> Shorten brings to the role something in limited supply within Labor: a capacity to effectively

prosecute a case. For all the criticism of Labor's union links and the structural limitations it places on party reform, the more effective unions continue to produce men and women trained to effectively argue a case publicly.

Some questioned whether the dispute-by-dispute approach of a seasoned union official produced the best result. When Shorten announced the final package of reforms in September 2011, it was declared something of a miracle that he had bridged the chasm between the parties. A version of MySuper had been agreed. Financial advisers were to be made more accountable to their clients than their masters. But the question remained: had Shorten gone too far to placate the retail funds? Everyone was more or less happy, but had he, in union jargon, "settled soft"?

Gillard reshuffled her cabinet in December. Support for her had fallen away and fresh storms were always on the horizon. The loss of a single supporter in the House might doom her government. Polls showed no great confidence she would be prime minister in a year's time. The reshuffle revealed how difficult her position was within the party. No great changes were made. Some ministers simply refused to budge. Shorten's promotion to cabinet as Minister for Employment and Workplace Relations was one

of the few changes that was plainly on merit. Shorten
had campaigned for the job. In the Qantas dispute
that led to the grounding of the whole fleet in October, he had outshone the minister he was replacing.
The press reported every move. It was a sign of his
growing strength that Gillard allowed him to keep
responsibility for superannuation while taking on
industrial relations. While this brought him into the
inner cabinet, it did not hand him any heavy reform
agenda. Gillard had seen off Howard's hated
WorkChoices, and while radical unions and big
industry complained about the new *Fair Work Act*,
Shorten's task was mainly to tinker and supervise. He
came into the job making his old boast that he could
work both sides of the aisle: "I don't believe it's too
difficult to be pro-employer and pro-employee at the
same time." Laura Tingle in the *Financial Review*
called the new minister "the union fox in the industrial relations chook shed."

Shorten had no doubt where his loyalties lay
when Rudd came for Gillard weeks after the reshuffle. Rudd had been briefing journalists and
whispering in caucus for months, but only broke
cover when an embarrassing little clip was posted on
YouTube. "This *fucking* language," he shouts, bang-
ing the table in frustration. "How can anyone do
this?" These were out-takes of the foreign minister

recording a video greeting in Mandarin. He is beside himself with rage. "Tell them to cancel this meeting at six o'clock. I haven't the fucking patience to go." With this humiliating clip on the net, Rudd offered himself to Sky; blamed Gillard's office for his embarrassment; and flew to Washington. Shorten might have stayed in the background, but found himself a few nights later on *Q&A*, where he denied rumours he was negotiating to be treasurer under a resurrected Rudd.

> I support the Prime Minister, for the same reasons that I supported her in June of 2010 and now. She is the best person for the job. She is the person who's strong. She's getting on with business ... She's had to negotiate legislation through a hung parliament, a minority government, and what she's managed to do is quite remarkable.

Finally Gillard and key ministers let Australia know what life with Kevin PM had been like. Shorten did not join this outpouring of scorn. He did not, as Nicola Roxon did, declare he would never serve under the man. Labor's candour did not sway Australia. Even as party leaders were dumping on Rudd, pollsters were told a switch to him would crush Abbott. Shorten and Conroy did the numbers for the prime minister in caucus. The AWU block of fifteen was solid. The entire union movement was backing her. When the vote came in late February 2012, she won by 71 votes to 31. Rudd promised never to challenge her again. He didn't pause.

It was a tainted year. In May, Shorten and his wife had to parade themselves in the *Herald Sun* under the headline "Our Love is Strong" to deny unspecified rumours – freely available on the net – of his infidelity. "Life's a journey of experiences," he told the paper. "I am in a good place right now and at the centre of that is the kids and Chloe." Labor accused the Opposition of spreading the gossip. Joe Hockey blamed the unions. Meanwhile, Peter Slipper had been ambushed with accusations – never proved – of sexual harassment. Opposition politicians were deeply involved in this attack on one of their own, a Liberal who had defected to become Speaker and thus shore up Gillard's government. The question was: could he continue in the role while civil action was pending against him? "These matters are for Mr Slipper to consider," Shorten declared. "I'm sure he's actually considering the question you asked very carefully." Gillard had other ideas: she needed Slipper where he was. There followed a famous exchange between Shorten and Sky's David Speers:

SPEERS: Do you think he should return to the Speaker's chair while the civil claims are still being played out?

SHORTEN: I understand the Prime Minister's addressed this in a press conference in Turkey in the last few hours. I haven't seen what she said, but let me say I support what it is that she's said.

SPEERS: Hang on. You haven't seen what she said ...

SHORTEN: But I support what my Prime Minister's said.

SPEERS: Well, what's your view?

SHORTEN: My view is what the Prime Minister's view is.

The comedy was undeniable. From distant London, the *Guardian* asked: "Is Bill Shorten the world's most loyal politician?" But veteran Canberra commentator Michelle Grattan saw the exchange rather differently: "Shorten was clearly distancing himself." Reports of the Slipper imbroglio were peppered with speculation that Shorten was positioning himself to challenge a crippled Gillard for the leadership. This was pure mischief. Poll after poll showed support for him taking her job didn't run into double figures.

Scandal followed scandal. Only days after the Slipper story broke, Shorten took the brawling Health Services Union to the Federal Court. Again, Gillard's survival was on the line, for at the heart of this sordid narrative was the member for Dobell and former general secretary of the union, Craig Thomson. Labor had protected him for as long as it could. The party had even contributed to his legal costs when he tried and failed to sue the Fairfax press over stories about him using his union credit card to buy sex. The end of the line was the report of an investigation into the union by Fair Work Australia that landed on Shorten's desk in early April. Thomson was cut loose from the Labor Party and sent to the crossbenches. Before releasing the 1000-page exposure of his corruption, Shorten announced the government would swiftly legislate to improve the financial oversight of unions, increase penalties and speed up investigations. The report revealed a fortune wasted on opulent living, prostitutes and funding Thomson's path to Canberra. The union had spent over $250,000 on his election alone. Shorten's response was to force the combined NSW, ACT and Victorian branches of the union into administration.

Action of this kind in the Federal Court had never been taken before. It earned him the ire of a very old political friend, the new national secretary of the union, Kathy Jackson. She called his move "a cheap political stunt." She too would be brought down in this squalid saga, but not before she inflicted some carefully calibrated damage on Shorten.

In an affidavit she couldn't persuade the court to accept, Jackson gave a spirited account of a confrontation with Shorten, one he denies ever took place. The scene was the party's Melbourne headquarters and the occasion a preselection contest for the marginal seat of Corangamite. According to the affidavit, Jackson had gone out for a cigarette when Shorten approached and asked her to back his candidate, Peter McMullin. Jackson says she refused:

JACKSON: I can't vote for him.

SHORTEN: Why not.

JACKSON: Because he is part of Spotless. Spotless have been screwing our outsourced members. I cannot vote for someone who is associated with a business that is screwing our members.

Jackson says the veins were showing in his forehead. "He said words loudly to the effect: 'You will fucking well vote for the candidate that I tell you to vote for. If you defy me, you will never be welcome in my home again and you will never have our support when you fucking well need it.'" McMullin wasn't preselected. Shorten threatened to sue the *Financial Review* if the story appeared. It was published in late June.

As if that were not enough filth to contend with, the sacked attorney-general, Robert McClelland, chose this moment to accuse his party of being soft on union corruption. "I know the Prime Minister is quite familiar with this area of the law," he said. "As lawyers in the mid-1990s, [we] were involved in a matter representing opposing clients." He was pointing to the old AWU scandals involving Gillard's then-partner Bruce Wilson. McClelland had been employed back then to try to claw money back from Wilson. The media took up the issue with renewed relish. Gillard repeated her old denials. Gun journalist at the *Australian* Hedley Thomas got to work, and a river of stories began flowing through the paper, seeking to tie Gillard to Wilson's frauds. Shorten did not back Gillard all the way. He condemned the slush fund she had set up for her boyfriend. "That account was unauthorised by the union," he told *Lateline*. "It was an inappropriate account. That account, as far as

I can tell, was out of bounds." Thomas and his team
wrote over 80,000 words, produced remarkable documents, showed young Gillard to have been a sloppy
lawyer, failed to implicate her in any crimes but did
the prime minister untold damage.

Rudd was circling all the time. The polls, which
seemed to be turning in Gillard's favour towards the
end of 2012, fell away in the new year. Shorten backed
Gillard unequivocally at the AWU conference in
February 2013 but more loudly than ever he was
being urged by the commentariat to abandon her.
The flattery of Rudd's people came with threats: be
king-maker now or never be king. Success had turned
Shorten into a trophy. So had his endless promotion
in the press as the leader down the track. He had
come to represent legitimacy within the party. The
faceless man of 2010 was the lieutenant both Gillard
and Rudd wanted seen by their side. The contest
between these rivals could be analysed as a battle
between old Labor and new; between a party of
unions and a party of civilians. But the contest was
really more personal, simpler and infinitely sad. This
was a battle between a man who couldn't do the job
and a woman who could; between a charismatic exile
and a leader deserted by the public; between a sabo-
teur who might win and an incumbent who seemed
not to have a hope.

Rudd made another fumbling attempt in March
2013. Shorten was conspicuously at Gillard's side
throughout the bizarre day when Rudd, in the end,
flinched from the contest. "It's been a big and event-
ful day," said Shorten in the aftermath. "We've got a
strong leader that's unanimously endorsed by her
team and I think the end of the day speaks for itself."
But the meaning of the day was slow to unfold. One
sign was the defection of Richard Marles to Rudd.
The ShortCons were not holding fast. Under the
extreme stress of the contest, the discipline of the factions was breaking down. It didn't help that despite
the great events in Canberra, the Right in Victoria
was feuding for the usual reason: a safe seat was on
the market. Nicola Roxon was leaving politics and
wanted a former staffer, Katie Hall, to have Gelli-
brand. Conroy wanted it for his staffer, Tim Watts. A
third contender was Kimberley Kitching, a one-time
Melbourne city councillor who had been hired to
clean up the HSU mess in Victoria. There was a
strong Shorten connection: Kitching was married to
his old friend, the blogger Andrew Landeryou. But
the women pulled out. Watts got the seat.

Cabinet did a good deal of soul-searching after
Rudd's second challenge. Shorten was still not a big
presence at the table. His focus remained on his portfolios and the factional hinterland. His superannuation

reforms had become law in 2012, and in early 2013 Jenny Macklin shepherded the National Disability Insurance Scheme through parliament. These were big achievements for which he could take a great deal of credit. But when he turned his mind in cabinet to the survival of the government, Shorten appeared to have little to contribute. One minister recalls:

> When governments are on the decline there comes a moment when the leader lets it run at cabinet and there's a debate. Now this is a government in trouble and Julia's opened it up for examination and there's some really good analysis from Tony Burke and Craig Emerson. I forget who else contributed. Do you know what Bill says? "Our senators aren't opening their offices in marginal seats. They've got their offices in the CBD." And I thought at the time, does he really believe this is even worth discussing here? You could have every Labor senator close his office in the central business district and move out to a marginal seat and it wouldn't make the faintest difference to the problems plaguing the Gillard government. It was the best he could come up with. I thought, if this is the guy who's being promoted as a future leader ...

Shorten was changing his mind about Gillard as the numbers flowed towards Rudd. He was deeply troubled. The AWU stood foursquare behind the prime minister and so did Conroy. For the first time in his political life, Shorten contemplated breaking with his closest allies. He admired and liked Gillard, but he had seen polling that suggested Labor's numbers in the House of Representatives would be halved if she led them to election day. He paid for a poll in Maribyrnong that showed a 13 per cent swing against him: this Labor prize would become marginal. There was no factional discipline in the drift towards Rudd. Individuals were making up their own minds. In some worlds, that's how politics works. Penny Wong had gone across. Kim Carr was happily behind Rudd again. The NSW Right was behind the contender and threatening to ignore Shorten in future leadership contests if he didn't shift too. Shorten was almost over the line. On Sunday 9 June, Barrie Cassidy set the contest ablaze by declaring on *Insiders* that Gillard would not be leading Labor to the next election. Swan would blame Shorten for lighting the match. Cassidy denies this. Shorten continued to maintain that he was backing the prime minister: "I support her and continue to support her." He saw Gillard just before the Midwinter Ball and told her how deeply concerned he was. He let her know the writing was on the wall. Convinced he had already switched, her people froze him out of strategic discussions. But Shorten says he vacillated almost until the last day:

> I hoped that this would pass, that somehow she would work it out, or he would work it out, or that they would work it out. Having been through one change I really did not want to be part of another change. No one has ever suggested I undermined Julia. My motivation seriously about the second change was a lot more thought-out, and a lot more difficult, and with a lot of scar tissue from the first change.
>
> I didn't think that Labor would win more than 25 or 30 seats if we stuck with Julia. I thought we were heading for Armageddon. My logic was that there are millions of people who put their trust in Labor and we had to come up with a better answer.

Shorten and Rudd met in Marles' office during the press gallery's Midwinter Ball on 19 June. Rudd was laying down conditions: he wouldn't save Labor from annihilation unless Shorten publicly backed his putsch. Both men disliked and distrusted each other. "Shorten wanted to hear Rudd make his case; he wanted to know Rudd was committed," Paul Kelly reports in *Triumph and Demise*. "Rudd, on the other hand, needed Shorten to sign up for change. Shorten had become a prize. But Shorten did not pledge to Rudd; he was too cautious, too distrustful." Asked a couple of days later on Melbourne radio by Neil Mitchell if he had discussed the leadership with Rudd, Shorten lied blind.

Gillard called on the contest on 26 June. She was all but certain she had lost the numbers. Shorten rang in the late afternoon to say he would be voting against her. She was not surprised. He only made his position public in the corridor outside the party room: "I have now come to the view that Labor stands the best chance to defend the legacy of this term of Parliament and to continue to improve the lives of millions of Australians with Kevin Rudd as our leader." He added: "I understand that this position that I have adopted may come at a personal cost to myself." He was all but alone. He had no faction behind him. His statement may have given comfort to waverers in caucus, but the head-counters of the party say Shorten brought only one other vote with him into the room. He didn't decide the issue but he was determined to own it. Why not just let it happen? "Because that's not leadership. A lot of other people didn't say what they were doing. But if I ever wanted to be a leader of this party, I didn't have the luxury of hiding."

Staying Put: 31 August 2015

Dyson Heydon brought only a couple of sheets of paper into the royal commission. His face was set. With dry formality he read a list of applications made, documents delivered and submissions received from half a dozen unions and the ACTU, asking him to stand down from his post. He spoke in the passive. It was as if he were somehow at a huge distance from himself. After five minutes he got to the point: "I have considered all the submissions. In my opinion the applications must be dismissed. I publish my reasons."

Shorten was still licking his wounds after his own appearance at the commission when news broke that Heydon was planning to give the annual Sir Garfield Barwick Address at a Liberal Party event in a Sydney city hotel. Marcus Priest, a sharp-eyed former journalist and adviser to Labor attorneys-general, had thought the flyer for the occasion peculiar: it was covered with advertising for the party and came with a form encouraging donations. Priest rang the New

South Wales Bar Association; they contacted Stoljar; he had a word to the commissioner next morning; and hours later the organisers of the dinner learnt His Honour would not, in fact, be giving the Liberal lawyers his views on "The Judicial Stature of Chief Justice Barwick Viewed in a Modern Perspective."

The news appeared to vindicate every accusation of bias Labor and the unions had leveled at the commission. Heydon would explain he'd cancelled the engagement "for sensible reasons of risk management and self-preservation," and "to avoid the attacks of the suspicious and the malicious." And they had poured down on his ancient head. Parliament was in uproar. Labor was triumphant. Abbott was again on the back foot, defending one of his pet projects. For Shorten, Labor and the unions, it was as if the sun had broken through a thick bank of cloud.

Heydon's account of how he got himself into this pickle was so like Shorten's evidence: he hadn't read the documents; matters were left to his staff; he wasn't across the detail; one or two crucial facts had slipped his mind; and no matter how bad things might appear, his integrity remained absolute. Most unlike Shorten was the political naivety of Heydon's 67-page exculpation. He could not be expected to admit the commission's task, while in some respects of high importance, was in others a political stitch-up. That would be to admit he should never have taken on the job. But in explaining his decision not to step down, Heydon made bizarre claims: that his was not an inquiry into the Labor Party, and the appearance of a former Labor prime minister and the current Labor leader of the Opposition had nothing to do with politics:

> Ms Gillard ... gave evidence not because she wanted to be or later became a Labor politician, but because a long time ago she acted as a solicitor for an official who was successively Western Australian State Secretary and Victorian State Secretary of the AWU ... I viewed her as a very good witness in almost all respects. Many, many findings favourable to her and rejecting the attacks of her numerous critics were made ...
>
> Similarly, Mr Shorten was not called to give evidence because of anything he did as a Labor politician ... the point is that assessment of what trade union officials did at a particular time is not affected either by their political role at those times or by their later adoption of a political career ...

Not canvassed by the old lawyer was the possibility that Gillard and Shorten may have been before him for the political purposes of the Liberal Party. There was no contest here between the government and the unions, he declared. His terms of reference expressed no animus towards trade unions. "They seek not to destroy unions or obstruct their purposes, but to see whether they have been fulfilled and to see how they might be better fulfilled in future."

And it was a wonder to watch the mighty machinery of his mind reach the conclusion that the dinner was not even a Liberal Party event. Though organised by two branches of the Liberal Party made up of lawyers; though described to Heydon as the flagship event of those branches; though the invitation came with advertising for the party and invitations to make political donations to the party; it could not be called a Liberal Party event "in any substantively useful sense," because it was also open to the public. Non-Liberals could come and listen to his "points of possible curiosity" about the former Chief Justice. Not being exclusively Liberal, the event was not Liberal at all.

Heydon recusing himself would have been a mighty victory for Shorten. This result was not a loss. Commentators were extraordinarily kind to the commissioner. Those who for days had been writing he had to go now declared it was inevitable he stay. His naive reasons were barely examined. News Corp swung heavily behind him. But an Essential Poll in late August found only one in four of those surveyed were willing to offer the commissioner much comfort. Dyson Heydon had lost a lot of paint. After slumping for months, Shorten's approval rating jumped ten per cent. Labor did not appeal the commissioner's decision but launched its attack on his findings which were still months away. Shorten declared: "Everything the royal commission says may as well have a Liberal Party logo stamped on it."

Faceless Man: 2013 to 2015

He is the master of a small room. This is a boardroom in a Sydney warehouse, where an outfit called BlueChilli aims to turn start-ups into businesses. It's as elegant as all get-out. Everyone is young. They're in a rush to go places even when they're standing still. Shorten is shown around: bare brick, coffee machines and whiteboards. He says: "Where's the ping-pong table?" The language around the table is twenty-first-century but the ask is as old as time: these tyro entrepreneurs want government help. Shorten is a convincing listener. His questions are sharp: "How does it make money?" When the jargon becomes opaque he calls for a translation. "Unicorns?" The one-in-a-million success. "Moon shoot?" The vision that electrifies a community. This idea seems to give him pause. He commits not a cent in that half-hour but farewells a happy room. "I promise we'll have a good policy, because you'll help to write it."

Shorten has been two years in the job. The mathematics were daunting when he began. In 2013 Labor suffered its worst defeat since the Depression. Rudd saved the party maybe fifteen seats but Shorten needs another twenty-two to govern. He insists he has no regret for the bloodletting that brought the party to this point: "We do retain the capacity to be an effective Opposition." There were good reasons for him not to seek the leadership. He was young. He had time. The Australian people barely knew him. And he knows how bleak the outlook is for leaders who take over once their party has been thrown out of office. A Labor veteran says:

> It's very hard to lead in Opposition. It's especially hard to lead in the first term after you've been in government. Your record of government is going to be flung back at you every day. The task of persuading the electorate that they were wrong three years ago is always very great if you look at history.
>
> You're really accepting a two-term strategy with deep confidence in your abilities to manage a disparate rumbling caucus and a bristling, insincerely loyal frontbench for six years. Faux matey-ness over the chopsticks. Gripes and grievances behind closed doors.

But the man who had for so long said he wanted to be leader could not back away. As much as anything, it was a question of credibility. If he flinched, how could he ever be believed again? On the Thursday after Rudd's defeat, Shorten called a press conference to confirm rumours he would be standing. The field was clearer than it might have been: Combet was ill and had left parliament. Chris Bowen, only forty, was willing to bide his time. But next day the Left's Anthony Albanese entered the contest. He was the favourite. A senior figure on the Right told Phil Coorey of the *Financial Review*: "Bill will get slaughtered."

What followed was the most civilised contest in Labor's history. Kevin Rudd's parting gift to the party was a radical protocol for making and breaking its leaders. After decades of empty talk about opening Labor to its members, something had finally been done. Under Rudd's new rules, hefty majorities of caucus would be needed to sack the leader: 75 per cent for a prime minister and 60 per cent for a leader of the Opposition. The plan was to outlaw ambush by faction. And when the time came for Labor to find a new leader, the rank and file would have an equal say with caucus. "The mechanisms," said Rudd, "prevent anyone from just wandering in one day, or one night, and saying, 'OK, sunshine, it's over.'"

For a month, the candidates were scrupulously polite to one another. They made almost identical policy pledges. Shorten suddenly discovered he had to extend his range, working out where he stood on issues that had barely troubled him in the past. Apart from differences over party reform – Albanese was calling on Labor to go further to break the power of the factions – the two were in such accord that the Left accused Shorten of deliberately "out Albo-ing Albo." To the commentators' surprise, Shorten won the set-piece debates comfortably. His opponent had stinging one-liners but Shorten found passion: "If I was to be PM, I would like to be known as the PM for the powerless, for the disempowered, for people who don't have a voice in society." Both men turned up at a barbecue breakfast in Perth to be questioned by officials of the CFMEU. Shorten pledged not to give back to the building industry watchdog, the Australian Building and Construction Commission, its old inquisitorial powers. "We like what you've said so far," remarked union official Joe McDonald. "Don't fuck it up."

Albanese won 18,230 rank-and-file votes. Shorten collected only 12,196 but had the numbers in caucus. "They broke arms and legs to lock in the vote for Shorten," said one veteran MP. The factions were still in disarray after Gillard's sacking, but the Right came together to back Shorten. A handful of Left MPs also drifted across to give him a big majority. His 64 per cent of the caucus outweighed Albanese's 60 per cent of the rank and file. Commentators made much of him not being the people's choice, but that caucus majority made him secure. There was no huge enthusiasm for him in the party. He was not seen as a miracle worker. But he was bricked in to the job. Yet his response to victory was drab. He barely celebrated. He seemed to shrink. Something had happened.

On the day he nominated for the leadership in September, a woman known as Kathy posted a message on Kevin Rudd's Facebook page, beneath his farewell message to the nation. She said Shorten "did things to me without my permission" at a camp in Portarlington twenty-seven years earlier. "You probably get crazy messages all the time," she wrote, "but I need help. Thankyou again for everything and I am sorry that the ALP did this to you too." The cartoonist Larry Pickering published her story on the net. Her allegations were detailed: she was sixteen, Shorten was nineteen, and a great deal of booze and some dope were involved the night she said he raped her in the bathroom of one of the cabins. She told Pickering she complained twice to the police: once in New South Wales in 2004, and again in Queensland in 2006 after she saw Shorten on television at Beaconsfield. She abandoned both complaints. Pickering believed her but was frank about her confusion and distress: "I assisted Kathy to her car and returned to my cramped office wondering how different Kathy's life might have been if Bill Shorten had never been born. To be honest, I am not certain it would have been."

The rape allegation was there all through the leadership contest and would remain unresolved for the first year of Shorten's leadership. In the bifurcated world of the modern media, he was named everywhere on the net but nowhere in the press. The Coalition showed remarkable tact. Shorten engaged one of Australia's smartest lawyers, Leon Zwier of Arnold Bloch Leibler, who issued blunt denials in November 2013 after the *Australian* published the first, careful story about "a senior Labor figure" accused of rape:

> Lawyers for the man said last night the "unsubstantiated claims date back almost 30 years and they have never previously been raised with him". "The unsubstantiated claims are absolutely without foundation and are distressing for his family and for him," the lawyers said. "He strongly denies any wrongdoing and will fully co-operate with any investigation. Police have not contacted him."

Shorten is tough. His eagerness and charm mask this but those who have worked with him over the years agree he is exceptionally resilient. But the rape allegation crushed him just as he was coming to grips with his new role. He had not, until this time, been a big figure in Labor's national affairs. He had a great deal to call on – his native skill as a recruiter, his talent for healing wounded institutions, his genius with numbers – but he also had a great deal to learn. Any leader comes to office with debts. Yet a lifetime of faction plays meant he had to feel his way forward with particular care. Shorten owed so much to so many. He aged. Something of his old panache disappeared. And in the new year, his mother suddenly died.

"I feel loss, and I feel I do not know when I will not feel loss," he said at her funeral a week later. His dedication to his mother was profound. All his life he has explained himself by talking about Ann McGrath – never his father, who kept the ships moving in and out of Duke and Orr, but the resolute girl from Ballarat who made her own future. His father had disappeared from their lives even before he abandoned his marriage when the boys were in their late teens. The son admits despising him. Shorten is one of that interesting pack of politicians born of determined mothers and largely absent fathers. There are so many: Barack Obama, Bill Clinton and Tony Blair are distinguished alumni. Among recent Labor leaders in Australia are Rudd, Albanese and Shorten. Among the qualities these men share are self-discipline, boundless ambition and an appetite for approval on a national scale.

The funeral at Xavier was a great gathering of family, academics and Labor leaders, with two priests in charge: Frank Brennan for the Catholics and the Shortens' Anglican from Moonee Ponds. "He did the homily," says Brennan, "and I did the mass." Shorten was stricken. Brennan saw "a very emotional, filial individual paying tribute to the public and private undertakings of a mother devoted to the cause of education as a source of justice for all."

She had raised her twins to be liked and to win. When he has to choose, Bill opts for winning but the tension between the two is old and deep. It leaves him hungry for reassurance. So many stories are told about Shorten the union official, the cabinet minister and the leader of the party asking: "How did I go?" He still wears the face his mother gave him, the face of a boy who wants to be liked. It's a charming mask that hides too much for his own good. This man would be more respected if, like Hawke, Keating and Howard, he let us see the bastard that's in there. Instead, the rough edges are politely hidden. Perhaps this is the instinct of a kid from not quite the right side of the tracks who lands in a place like Xavier. "Don't let your heads be turned," Ann told her boys. She meant that. "She believed in merit," Shorten said at the funeral. "She taught me that merit is a legitimate human condition. That people should not be deified because of some ill-defined birth right or the wealth of an individual." But she also taught her sons to be polite and careful, to be good boys. There is about Shorten still a faint sense that he is a suitor in the world he wants to lead.

For a time he retreated to mourn. Months later, a photograph of his mother was on the fridge when Annabel Crabb brought the *Kitchen Cabinet* crew to Moonee Ponds for the awkward business of watching him cook ratatouille. Talking about Ann led him naturally to another big issue in his life: rivalry. "I thought my brother must have been better at the piano for no other reason than I thought it," he said, stirring the eggplant for the cameras. "When you're a twin, of course you never compete." He was delighted to bump into his old piano teacher Joyce Haslem at the funeral. "I said to Joyce, who was better at the piano? And Joyce said, not my brother. I haven't told him that. I realise it's naughty of me. It's naughty." He laughs like a little boy. Shorten is deeply competitive. Beating a staffer at five hundred fills him with glee.

On *Kitchen Cabinet* he gave the impression that his mother was, along with everything else, the presiding genius of competition in his life. A few years before her death, talking to News Corp's Andrew Rule, she delivered a gnomic assessment of her two boys:

> At the end of a couple of hours, the conversation turned back to her sons. Rob, the quiet and steady banker, was more like her side of the family, she thought. And Bill, the mercurial one? She thought about it a while, rubbing her old dog's ears then said, "Bill … Bill is more like his father."

After ten months' investigation and on advice from the Office of Public Prosecutions, Victoria Police decided not to lay charges: "There was no reasonable prospect of conviction." The *Australian* broke the story on 21 August under the headline "Labor figure cleared in rape case." Kathy told reporter Dan Box, "How am I feeling? Angry, really, really angry." That afternoon, Shorten held a press conference to identify himself as the accused Labor figure:

> I fully co-operated to clear my name. And that is what I have done … the police have now concluded the investigation. The decision speaks for itself. It is

over … I think in all fairness I have the right to draw the line on this. I have no intention of making any further comment.

Shorten's colleagues rallied around him. In October Kathy engaged Melbourne QC Peter Faris and there was talk of her bringing a civil suit. That has not materialised and Shorten believes there is no prospect that it will. Lawyers say the closer the elections, the greater the risk the courts would regard any suit as an abuse of process. Coalition attack ads have not alluded in any way to Kathy's allegation. They don't emerge even in hostile focus groups. They are not part of the contest.

Abbott chose to fight Shorten on trust. Ipsos, Newspoll and Essential all agreed that Australians found the Labor leader a great deal more understanding than his opponent, far more broad-minded, steadier and a deeper thinker. But they distrusted him almost as much as they distrusted the prime minister. In Question Time in late August 2015 Abbott let rip:

That smirking phoney over there, that assassin, the two-time Sussex Street assassin … Twice this Leader of the Opposition led the Sussex Street death squads to assassinate politically two prime ministers, and then he was caught out telling lies about it on the Neil Mitchell program. That is this person who now seeks the trust of the Australian people at the next election ... We support the workers of this country. Where does this man stand? I tell you: when it comes to dudding workers, that man has form. He wants to dud the workers of Adani, he wants to dud the workers who will be employed under the free trade agreement, but, worst of all, when he was charged with protecting low-paid workers, he ripped them off to help himself. Shame on him.

Australians had their doubts about both men but knew which party they preferred to govern the country. From the moment of the Coalition's victory there crept over the nation what the pollster Andrew Catsaras calls "a sombre mood of buyer's remorse." Regret and disillusionment coloured the country's politics under Abbott. Nearly every poll from late 2013 showed Australia ready to go back to Labor. That verdict was Shorten's principal political asset. He had Abbott on his side. His leadership was secure. He hadn't set Australia on fire, but in the eyes of his colleagues he was doing well. He'd found his feet. His critics in the party called him workman-like. He had not made many mistakes. "I know there is more goodwill towards me at the moment in the party than there has been," he says. "It develops over time."

In the winter of 2015, I had coffee with him in a Sydney café. He has a sweet tooth and a little gut to match. He jogs, and he shows me an app that records his laps round Canberra's parliamentary triangle. He's fitter now than he seems in old footage of his union days and reckons he's beaten Abbott once or twice on fun runs. The idea pleases him. But he wants a serious word: "If your yarn is about Bill Shorten the factional operator, I don't think that really captures what's going on. It's part of my history I've worked through. But you know, the games are not worth doing if they're just for the sake of the games."

Shorten is still a player. The Stability Pact nearly came apart at Gillard's execution. Shorten was punished. All of his picks for parliamentary real estate in the 2013 election were foiled. Gillard's seat he wanted to go to Andrew Landeryou's wife, Kimberley Kitching. Gillard blocked that. He then tried to put Kitching into the Senate. Conroy blocked that. His candidate for Simon Crean's old seat lost out when both Conroy and the NUW both sided against him. Since that time, Shorten and Conroy have made up. These days it's more a marriage of convenience, but the ShortCons are back in action. The Stability Pact is tightening its grip on the factions. They are as quiet as they have been in living memory – too quiet according to Labor veterans who mourn the loss of creative friction inside the party. And the numbers games go on, more ferociously than ever as party membership and union membership dwindle. Talent is finding it even harder to beat the machine.

He's in a big-picture mood. There's a book on the way. Memoirs? "No, what I stand for." When he riffs about his politics, he doesn't use the language of the shop floor or the hustings. It's faintly New Age: "I fundamentally believe that if you empower people, you can move mountains. I fundamentally believe that if people are given a fair go, the world's a better place, people are happier individually and society progresses." He says he's grown. "I've learnt along the way. I'm a different person at forty-eight than I was at twenty-eight and certainly different to who I was at eighteen." So what does he know now that he didn't know then? "First, you've got to back yourself in. You don't wait for everyone else to agree, because that's not the way of progress. Second, I always ask myself: what will this look like in ten years' time? You worry about tomorrow, but you've got to ask: what will this look like in ten or twenty years' time?"

Not for the first time in these weeks, Shorten talks Napoleon. It is surprising how often he cites military rather than political thinkers. He tells me he admires John Monash for carrying out such meticulous preparation before every attack on the Western Front. But Napoleon is his hero and over coffee he once again cites the Corsican's maxim: find your enemy's weakest point and concentrate your attack there. That would be Tony Abbott. Yet the question hanging over Shorten at this time was whether he had, in fact, taken the fight up to Abbott. In the rolling catastrophe of the Coalition government, most of the damage done to the prime minister has been self-inflicted. Another of Napoleon's maxims comes to mind: never interfere with an enemy in the process of destroying himself.

Shorten is by instinct a deal-maker. This explains a good deal of the difficulty he faces cutting through as leader of the Opposition. At the AWU he stacked on disputes and they could be willing. But the point was always to settle. And he was known then – and later as a minister – for reaching settlements that left all sides reasonably happy. His critics say he settles soft. If the top job is ever his, being a fine networker, recruiter and deal-maker will stand Shorten in great stead. But getting there is a different matter. A leader of the Opposition's task is to cultivate division. Abbott proved a genius at that. But Shorten struggles often to subdue the agreement demon in his nature.

He has defined differences between the sides. He has defended Medicare, pensioners, the unemployed and university students. He is a republican who backs equal marriage. Labor under Shorten has pledged to continue the fight against climate change:

> We were right to support an emissions trading scheme. We were right to establish the Climate Change Authority, the Clean Energy Finance Corporation and the Australian Renewable Energy Target. For this, we do not apologise. From this, we do not resile. We are not sceptics. We believe in the science.

But where Abbott was most himself, Shorten beat a retreat. "For Labor, national security is – and always will be – above politics," he says but what he means is that Labor will buckle whenever the government declares security is at stake. No political capital will be spent protecting liberty and the rule of law. Labor has tinkered with Abbott's security legislation but in the end has supported every measure: for the retention of metadata; prison for reporting ASIO "special" operations; broadening the already wide offence of "advocating" terrorism; retaining control and preventative detention orders; and stripping dual nationals of their Australian citizenship without trial or conviction.

What will it look like in ten years' time, I ask, that Labor passed a law to throw doctors and nurses in prison for reporting what they see on Manus and Nauru? "We will stand by them," he replies indignantly. But Labor voted for the Border Force Act and that's exactly what it does. "I don't share that interpretation." This is utterly baffling. Once dragged into court, nurses and social workers may have some whistle-blower protection but Labor voted to drag them there. Labor has voted for secrecy. Shorten has no idea how the camps will be cleared. He acknowledges that endorsing pushbacks at the National Conference in July 2015 was only the latest in a long line of catch-ups with the Coalition's refugee policies. But he is confident Labor won't be forced to go any further: the worst has been reached. But isn't that what Labor always says? "Time will tell but I know that if we want more humanity in our system, I'll do a better job than the other fellow."

Weeks later, a wave of mockery compelled the Australian Border Force to abandon Operation Fortitude – a plan to send its gorgeously uniformed officers out to check the visa status of "any individual we cross paths with" in the streets of Melbourne. Did Shorten speak for the nation when he heard about this scheme? No, he spoke for a party terrified of the wedge. "If you're going to do a blitz," he said solemnly, "I don't know why you'd necessarily tele-graph it to the media first." Demonstrators rallied at Flinders Street station, and within a couple of hours Operation Fortitude was canned. Only then did Shorten find his voice to condemn "one of the most catastrophically silly ideas I've seen this government do ... I don't think there's a single Victorian and indeed a single Australian whose jaw just didn't hit the ground ... truly, how dumb is this government some days?" Once he was safe, he was magnificent.

In the end, Abbott didn't wash with Australia. He was a brawling politician of great skill but also – and fatally – still so much the Cold War kid who rode out with Bob Santamaria's men in the late 1970s to con-front the zeitgeist and save Western civilisation. "The beauty of being leader is you are freer to be yourself," Abbott remarked after becoming leader of the Oppo-sition. But that self proved, in the end, not made for the politics of today. He never lost his old mentor's fear of the future and the belief that his mission was to save us from enemies we never imagined were there. Abbott was only Santa lite, but in the end he failed where Santamaria failed half a century earlier: we didn't buy their vision of a nation in peril. We don't see ourselves that way.

Turnbull came for Abbott in mid-September. He did not make Julia Gillard's mistake. Nothing was wrapped in euphemism. He blasted the man out of office. Next day in the House, Shorten did his chores. He attacked the "reactionary, fractured government" of the old prime minister and the grip Abbott's policies would have on Turnbull, just returned from the morning's ceremonies at Yarralumla: "Last night the change was all about the style. It was about panicked MPs worrying about their job security and not thinking about the jobs of Australians. There is nothing of substance which will change in this government."

The Rise of Modern Man: 2016

A dance hall on a busy street not far from Sydney's Central Station has for decades done hard yards in the service of experimental theatre and stand-up comedy. One night in March, the *Guardian Australia* rented the place for a forum on equal marriage. The platform was crowded with campaigners, comedians and politicians. Turning out for the event was every letter of the GLBTI alphabet. Shorten was there with his wife, Chloe, who cut a vivid figure even in that crowd in a leopard-skin raincoat. Shorten was entirely at ease.

He has brought the party a long way. I remember sitting with Gillard's dour tactician John McTernan in early 2013 as he tried to convince me Labor could beat Abbott by campaigning as the modern party. "What about equal marriage?" I asked. McTernan was silent. The issue was already totemic, a pointer to which century a political party was operating in, but the branch of the Catholic Church known as the Shop, Distributive and Allied Employees' Association had used its great muscle to stack parliament with men and women prepared to die in a ditch for traditional marriage. Shorten changed that. Behind the scenes at the Labor conference in Melbourne in 2014 he bluntly told the Shoppies equal marriage was going to happen. No rebellion followed. Meanwhile, the Coalition was tearing itself apart on the issue. Turnbull might once have been on the dance-hall platform in March with Shorten and the leader of the Greens, Richard Di Natale. Not now. Backtracking on equal marriage has done the prime minister great damage in middle Australia. Labor's strategic dream in 2013 has become reality in 2016: in this contest, Shorten is leading the modern party.

He had a story for the rally. That morning at an RAAF wreath-laying ceremony he had been accosted by a little old lady who cried, "God will damn you for your position on marriage equality." Then she slipped him a note: "And your child's undisciplined too." In language you don't expect Labor leaders to use, Shorten gave busybodies a spray:

> People judging lesbian or gay or bisexual or transgender relationships are actually judging more than just those groups. They are judging the single parents; they are judging the people who have got divorced. I live in a blended family. I

have stepchildren who I regard as my own children. So this is the point I think that we are seeing: the face of what constitutes a family is changing. Good luck to people who have never been divorced. But do you know what? If you've been divorced, you're an equally worthy human being. And children are raised not just by same-sex couples but raised in blended families.

The good news is – and this is why there is change in the Labor Party, quite significant change in a relatively short time – that we know now that families come in all shapes and sizes. I bitterly resent when I hear some people judging other relationships. Until you are in that relationship, until you are raising those children, get out of my life. I don't want your opinions … I represent a whole lot of Australians who in the last ten years have started waking up and thinking about it and being touched by personal stories. The good news is that the religious right no longer owns the definition of what a family is. And they can't win.

The bookies aren't betting Shorten can win either. That he might emerge this year as prime minister hasn't gripped the national imagination. No one is asking the Labor leader what he will do in his first hundred days. But in late summer, as the polls swung back in Labor's favour, even hostile commentators agreed: Shorten can't be ruled out. They had been wrong so often, as blow after blow failed to knock him out. He survived Dyson Heydon. He survived the rise of Malcolm Turnbull. He survived the last polls of 2015 that put the Coalition's two-party-preferred vote at 53 per cent and Labor's at 47 per cent. By late February, Newspoll and Essential had the parties level-pegging. Shorten admits he didn't predict this. "But I didn't predict I was going to be wiped out either."

Heydon might have ended Shorten's career. But he announced in November that he would not be levelling charges of criminal or unlawful conduct against the leader of the Opposition. Shorten marked his acquittal not with expressions of gratitude to the old High Court judge but with a fresh attack on this "politically motivated royal commission, set up by the Liberal Party to throw mud and smear its political opponents." After consulting his old mentor Bill Kelty and his union rival Greg Combet, Shorten proposed a number of reforms to make union leadership more accountable: "Labor does have zero tolerance for criminality and illegality." The modest attention these plans earned was overwhelmed by the release on New Year's Eve of Heydon's final report, with its denunciation of union "louts, thugs, bullies, thieves,

perjurers, those who threaten violence, errant fiduci-
aries and organisers of boycotts." Though spared the
prospect of prosecution, Shorten had to deal with the
commissioner's focus on the AWU as a case study of
failings uncovered across the wider union movement:
the creation of false records, the soliciting of large
sums from employers, and the false inflation of membership numbers:

> When several of these themes are taken together, a
> sinister picture appears to form. It is a picture of
> the union concerned not with its role as the instru-
> ment through which to protect the interest of its
> members but with self-interest. Its primary inter-
> est is in the leading group of its officials as a
> self-perpetuating institution. The institution
> comes to operate like a Venetian oligarchy or a
> Whig Parliament with very few electoral contests.
> It is an institution more concerned with gathering
> members than servicing them.

He recommended a slew of charges be laid against
Shorten's successor at the helm of the AWU and
many company officers with whom he'd done deals.
All protested their innocence.

Shorten and his family went to ground for a fortnight at Bawley Point. Mobile reception is poor on

that stretch of the NSW south coast. He kept to his new health regime: "High protein, low carbs. No tummy tucking or Chinese herbal medicine. I'm just doing it the old-fashioned way." He read war histories and heroic biographies of Martin Luther King, Columbus and the coach of the Green Bay Packers, Vince Lombardi. He worked on the narrative of his renewal. "I didn't think all hope was lost at the end of 2015," he says. "I knew that a lot of the policy work we're doing was ready to go – costings, policy, the themes." Labor under Shorten was ignoring the ground rule of Australian politics that Oppositions must present to their opponents as small a target as possible for as long as possible. "I want Labor to provide a serious, positive alternative," he says. "For Labor to form a government, we cannot rely on Coalition torpor and mistakes. We've ripped up the rule book." At a supermarket in Queanbeyan on his first day back at work in mid-January he declared, "I believe it's important that we rule the line under 2015 and start 2016 being upfront and straight with the Australian people about our policies. I can promise Australians that we'll do a better job in health care and education, that we will stand up for Australian jobs and that we are fair dinkum about acting on climate change."

Australia wasn't listening. The party was gloomy. Polls taken in the last days of January showed Labor was still facing a wipe-out. Faction leaders in New South Wales and Victoria began to take soundings. Shorten's leadership was under pressure. Albanese was seen as the only alternative. Murmurings of disquiet reached the press. But as Shorten was being told to lift his game, the Coalition began to implode. In early February, Turnbull abandoned plans to raise the GST rate. The one big, brave idea he had been promoting for months was cast aside. The following week, Shorten announced that Labor would radically restrict tax benefits for negative gearing on investment properties. This was brave. Tinkering with negative gearing had proved electoral poison for Labor in the past. Shorten's stature grew in the hectic days that followed, as Turnbull mocked and then dismissed any prospect of the government backing such a reform. Polls taken as that contest raged showed the government and Opposition suddenly neck and neck.

"I thought that when Malcolm Turnbull took over that politics would be harder for us, but politics might be better overall and it would be an opportunity for everyone to lift their game," says Shorten. "When you play a better or a smarter opponent, it forces you to work harder, doesn't it? ... what has surprised me is that the government has crumpled inwards." Shorten found himself facing an opponent easier to grapple with. "Abbott is a master at turning a stick into a club. He is a puncher. Turnbull talks too much, doesn't focus enough. I don't know if he's match-fit. I don't get the impression he's clear what he wants to do." While the government talks house-keeping – shifting the tax mix, attending to the deficit – Labor is talking policy. It may be crazy-brave. Billions are at stake backing Gonski and the National Disability Insurance Scheme in the years ahead. But fading fast as Labor's policies come under attack from the government is the old image of Shorten as a shapeshifter interested only in power.

Playing strongly to his advantage is Turnbull's shift away from the constant wedging of Labor on national security. The humiliations Shorten accepted to prevent his party being branded as soft on terror-ism seem – at least for the moment – a thing of the past. He looks more like a leader as a result. These days the rule-of-law arguments he might have raised in defence of Muslim Australians, refugees and whistleblowers he deploys to defend unionists who might fall foul of a re-empowered Australian Build-ing and Construction Commission. "The ABCC should deal with ordinary industrial laws, not crimi-nal matters. But the government's given it extraordinary coercive powers on the back of Dyson Heydon's Royal Commission ... powers more draconian to deal with tradies on Australian building sites than for police or courts handling ice trafficking or terrorism."

Shorten cuts a different figure these days. The body language is not as exaggerated. He has abandoned his most irritating pose: faux-thoughtful. His brows are no longer theatrically creased for the cameras. The serious face he presents now looks like his own. He's looking for his old voice, the one he had before he went into parliament. "What I'm trying to do is talk to people and make sure our polices are speaking to their future. I'm very clear now. I feel I have a clarity of purpose that has been two-and-a-half years in the making." He's asserting his authenticity. In March he told the Press Club:

> I'm a unionist, I'm Labor, I'm a husband, I'm a father. I believe in the Republic and I believe in marriage equality ... I'm an internationalist ... I describe myself as the descendant of convicts and the descendant of unsuccessful goldminers, and my dad was a fitter and turner and then became a ships engineer ... a seafarer. My mum was a teacher and became a university lecturer. I don't have to pretend to be who I'm not. My Labor Party doesn't have to pretend who it is not. Isn't that one of the great challenges of leadership? It is hard to

lead a nation when you have to pretend to be something that you're not.

This doesn't make Shorten charismatic. The polls are his friend. The nation is treating him with respect. The press is not on his side but is giving him a better run. But he does not command attention. Shorten's arrival doesn't light up a room. A hard rule of the last half-century has been that it takes a larger-than-life figure to bring Labor in from Opposition. Whitlam, Hawke and Rudd were such men. Shorten doesn't claim to be in their league. When I raise the charisma question, he laughs it away. He doesn't like it. Who would? "See how we go in the debates with Malcolm," he says. But do we pay enough attention to debates? "You will."

We've met on a hot Sydney autumn afternoon at roughly the 900-day mark of his leadership of the Opposition. He's fond of the figure, which crops up again and again in our conversation: "We've spent 900 days working on what we think we should do ..." I observe it's a strange sort of a job being leader of the Opposition: whoever has it wants desperately to be rid of it. Shorten cuts me off: "It's the job before the one you want, but in my opinion the only way to get to the job you want is to do the job you've got." There's something of the flavour of Xavier in the way he talks up the value of the long grind of Opposition. "You can't know what this job is on the first day. What you learn about being an Opposition leader is acquired over time, from scars, with lessons, with talking to people, with what governments do, how your party organises its ideas. To anyone who came to me and said, 'One day I'd like to be prime minister,' I would say to them, 'First you must be Opposition leader, because the lessons you're learning now will make you a better prime minister.' I can't say I've enjoyed every day of Opposition, but I can say that I think I'm a better leader for every day I've had."

Australian politics are said to be volatile. Really, they're repetitive. The same stories are told, the same scenes recur again and again with only a switch of cast. It's as if the system itself is incapable of learning. We find ourselves in so many ways where we were in Gillard's time. An Opposition leader not much loved faces a prime minister under attack from within. There was at least an argument last time that restoring Rudd might revive the fortunes of his party. Not a skerrick of such hope attaches to Abbott. The government is restive. The Opposition is disciplined. Again the country wonders if an Opposition leader can rise above the narrow politics that brought him to the top. There's no doubt Bill Shorten would have made a fine premier of Victoria. But can he scale up?

"I look forward to demonstrating that," he says. "I know what the nation should look like in ten and fifteen years' time and it's up to me to tell that story to the nation. My job isn't to convince Malcolm Turnbull or News Limited that they should vote for me. My job is to convince Australians I have a plan for the future."

2 MAY 2016

Sources

Bill Shorten gave me time and documents, for which I am most grateful. Colleagues from his many lives – schoolboy to leader of the Opposition – helped me on and off the record to grasp the shape of his complicated life.

But this essay would not have been possible without the labour over many years of my colleagues, particularly in the Melbourne press, who tracked the wild factional plays that are at the heart of Shorten's career. Of that big team, I want to thank particularly Jason Koutsoukis, Ewin Hannan, Brad Norington and the splendid Michael Bachelard. At the end of my desk is a wall of books about the Rudd–Gillard era. Over the last months I have regularly given thanks for the memoirs of Gillard, Combet and Rob Oakeshott; the diaries of Bob Carr; Paul Kelly's *Triumph and Demise*, Aaron Patrick's *Downfall* and Barrie Cassidy's *The Party Thieves*.

Russell Marks, lawyer and policy advisor, recruited his La Trobe colleague Dominic Kelly, doctoral candidate and political commentator, to a two-man research team of great skill and endless energy. They were my seeing-eye dogs in the dark world of Victorian politics.

And this is something I've never done before: thank Chris Feik, my infinitely demanding editor at Black Inc., for dragging another Quarterly Essay out of me.

Transcripts for the Royal Commission into Trade Union Governance and Corruption can be accessed at www. tradeunionroyalcommission.gov.au/Hearings/Documents/

Sources

Transcripts/2015/Transcript-8-July-2015.pdf (8 July) and www.
tradeunionroyalcommission.gov.au/Hearings/Documents/
Transcripts/2015/ Transcript-9-July-2015.pdf (9 July).

1   "I'm stuffed": *Saturday Paper*, 12 December 2015, p. 15.

4   "Bill is different": Bill Kelty to me, 22 July 2015.

8   "I have suggested": William Shorten, Royal Commission on
         the Activities of the Federated Ship Painters and Dockers
         Union, 3 February 1981, p. 754.

8–10   "Look it up", "Because it's quicker", "There was politics"
         and "The breadth of": Shorten's eulogy for his mother,
         15 April 2014, text supplied by Shorten.

10   "This, from the beginning": Letter from Fr Pedro Arrupe
         SJ, 20 May 1978, *Xaverian* (Xavier College), December
         1978, p. 5.

11   "Don't let your heads be turned": Shorten's eulogy,
         15 April 2014.

11   "outstanding contribution" and "William proved":
         Xaverian, 1983, pp. 30 & 39.

12   "He was always": Chris Gleeson to me, 23 June 2015.

12   "We were all very": John Roskam to me, 24 June 2015.

12   "The house meetings": *Xaverian*, 1984, p. 28.

13   "I've always been" and all other quotations from Des King:
         To me, 6 July 2015.

13   "He is breaking": Race Mathews to me, 25 June 2015.

14   "I was a": "Insight", *Age*, 24 September 2009, p. 1.

14   "I chose to": Shorten to me, 16 July 2015.

14   "I wasn't really": Shorten to me, 30 July 2015.

14–15   "Our spies also": *Lot's Wife*, 7 September 1985, p. 15.

15   "In reply to": *Lot's Wife*, vol. 25, no. 8, p. 15.

16 "The Socialist Left": *Sunday Age*, 28 May 2006, p. 13.

16 "Network had one": Aaron Patrick, *Downfall: How the Labor Party Ripped Itself Apart*, ABC Books, 2013, p. 13.

16 "Bill was just": Patrick to me, 21 July 2015.

17 "Get all your mates" and "It was about": Peter Cowling to me, 24 June 2015.

18 "A sport where": *Sunday Age*, 28 May 2006, p. 13.

18–19 "In your last": *Lot's Wife*, 28 July 1986, p. 27.

19 "a festival of" and "spiteful screaming matches": *Lot's Wife*, 23 June 1986, p. 7.

20 "I know they say": Shorten to me, 30 July 2015.

20 "legitimate market research": *Lot's Wife*, 15 June 1987, p. 3.

20–1 "We lobbied", "That was somthing" and "No. No.": Shorten to me, 30 July 2015.

22–3 "They spent a couple": Patrick, *Downfall*, p. 19.

22 "As a former Young": Christina Cridland, *Sunday Times*, Perth, 16 June 2013, p. 67.

23 "You can't keep": Shorten to me, 30 July 2015.

24 "Politics is a": Shorten to me, 30 July 2015.

24 "We were cheesed": Information to me.

24 "I enjoyed his": Julia Gillard, *My Story*, Knopf, 2014, p. 417.

24–5 "He was active" and "John Cain Junior": Testimony of Robert Kernohan to the Royal Commission into Trade Union Governance and Corruption, 11 June 2014, www.tradeunionroyalcommission.gov.au/Hearings/Documents/Transcripts/turc-transcript-public-hearing-11june2014.pdf, pp. 369 & 370.

25–8 "From the time" and all other Peter Koutsoukis quotes: To me, 7 July 2015.

26 "A lawyer with": *Age*, 2 April 1994, p. 1.

26 "Mr Kernohan said": *Financial Review*, 9 July 1992, p. 4.

27 "Where someone has": Shorten to me, 8 July 2015.

Sources

27–8   "He was very young" etc.: Bill Kelty to me, 22 July 2015.

28   "When I was": *Hansard*, 14 February 2008, p. 328.

30   "to shine": Tony Abbott, joint press conference, 10 February 2014, www.pm.gov.au/media/2014-02-10/joint-press-conference-attorney-general-and-minister-employment-parliament-house.

31   "Instead of securing": Jeremy Stoljar, Counsel Assisting Opening Statement, Royal Commission, 28 May 2015, www.tradeunionroyalcommission.gov.au/Hearings/Documents/Transcripts/2015/Transcript-28-May-2015.pdf, p. 7.

32   "I thought it was": Ben Davis's testimony, Royal Commission, 4 June 2015, www.tradeunionroyalcommission.gov.au/Hearings/Documents/Transcripts/2015/Transcript-4-June-2015.pdf, p.648.

32   "dudding their workers": *Alan Jones Breakfast Show*, Radio 2GB, 11 June 2015, www.pm.gov.au/media/2015-06-11/interview-alan-jones-radio-2gb-sydney.

34   "There is no way" and "I don't micromanage": Shorten's testimony, Royal Commission, 8 July 2015, pp. 58 & 16.

34   "I don't know" and "I would never": Shorten's testimony, 9 July 2015, pp. 59 & 113.

35–6   "You, if I can" and "You may or": Dyson Heydon, Royal Commission, 9 July 2015, pp. 136 & 201.

36   "This hurt him": Kelty to me, 22 July 2015.

37   "The old AWU": Shorten to me, 8 July 2015.

38   "A lot of people": *Age*, 3 April 1995, p. 8.

38   "We are all": *Age*, 19 June 1997, p. 18.

39   "It wasn't doable": Shorten to me, 30 July 2015.

39–40   "Shorten cut me": Kernohan's witness statement, par. 134.

40   "He has had": Royal Commission into Trade Union Governance and Corruption Interim Report, vol. 1, par. 294, www.tradeunionroyalcommission.gov.au/reports/Documents/InterimReportVol1.pdf.

Sources

40–1   "Do the people" and "Steve Bracks said": Shorten to me, 8 July 2015.

41   "I could have": Patrick, *Downfall*, p. 190.

41–2   "I listen to" etc.: Shorten to me, 30 July 2015.

42   "You've got to be": Kelty to me, 22 July 2015.

43   "Trade union officials": *BRW*, 14 December 1998, p. 46.

44   "Esso makes $1 million": *Age*, 31 July 2001, p. 2.

44   "a mixture of": *Herald Sun*, 21 April 2001, p. 27.

45   "It's like bringing": *Herald Sun*, 24 March 2000, p. 20.

45   "The first thing": *Herald Sun*, 21 April 2001, p. 27.

46   "Shorten, who is": *BRW*, 22 June 2001, p. 18.

47   "You're asking for": Shorten's testimony, 9 July 2015, pp. 128–9.

47   "Whilst I was": Shorten's testimony, 8 July 2015.

47–8   "What profoundly weakens": Shorten's testimony, 9 July 2015, p. 189.

48   "Generally speaking": Stoljar, 28 May 2015, p. 6.

49   "Are you able" etc.: Stoljar and Shorten, 8 July 2015, p. 103.

49   "Carries a risk": Final report of the Royal Commission into Trade Union Governance and Corruption, vol. 4, ch. 10.2, par. 372.

50   "If you and I": Shorten's testimony, 8 July 2015, p. 82.

50–1   "If it was the case": Heydon's final report, vol. 4, ch. 10.2, par. 45.

51   "side-stepped the scrutiny": Heydon's final report, vol. 4, ch. 10.2, par. 47.

51   "presented with misleading": Heydon's final report, vol. 4, ch. 10.2, pars 65 and 66.

51   "highly unlikely that": Shorten's testimony, 8 July 2015, p. 65.

51–2   "Nothing untoward about" and "Unions have been": Shorten's testimony, 9 July 2015, pp. 126 & 121.

52   "This is a long way": *Sydney Morning Herald*, 27 October 2003, p. 6.

52   "If the company": Shorten's testimony, 9 July 2015, pp. 126 & 117.

52–3   "It was the idea": Shorten's testimony, 8 July 2015, p. 87.

53   "I had a lot": Shorten's testimony, 9 July 2015, p. 156.

53   "The best way": Shorten's testimony, 8 July 2015, p. 86.

54   "The payments were made": Heydon's final report, vol. 4, ch. 10.5, par. 92(c).

55   "substantial involvement": Heydon's final report, vol. 4, ch. 10.5, par. 91.

55   "Anything that we raised": Shorten's testimony, 9 July 2015, p. 193.

55   "Payments for paid" and "deposited into the AWU": Heydon's final report, vol. 4, ch. 10.4, pars 29 & 25.

56   "Tollway workers": *Age*, 10 March 2005, p. 9.

56   "It was a big": Shorten's testimony, 9 July 2015, p. 114.

57   "no suggestion": Heydon's final report, vol. 4, ch. 10.3, par.220.

57   "That would and could": Shorten's testimony, 9 July 2015, p. 137.

58   AWU ball etc.: MFI – 9, Thiess John Holland, Royal Commission, evidence presented, 9 July 2015.

58   "I cannot speak", "could always be" and "research work done": Shorten's testimony, 9 July 2015, pp. 123, 118 & 112.

58–9   "Back strain" etc.: Stoljar and Shorten, 9 July 2015, p. 118.

60   "They were no more": Heydon's final report, vol. 4, ch. 10.3, par. 218.

60   "a very good": Shorten, 9 July 2015, p. 113.

62–8   "A lot of" and all other Shaun Micallef quotes: To me, 29 July 2015.

63–8   "I'd Like to Teach the World to Zing": Script provided by Shaun Micallef.

Sources

66   "It is like": *Hansard*, 9 February 2015, p. 80.

66   "These people opposite" and "Treasurer Hockey": *Sydney Morning Herald*, 2 December 2014.

66   "If I can borrow": *Australian*, 17 January 2015, p. 20.

67   "We have now": *Australian*, 22 January 2015, p. 9.

69   "And the last": *Australian*, 20 September 2005, p. 2.

70   "How low can": Mark Latham, *The Latham Diaries*, MUP, 2005, p. 138.

71   "It was the beginning": Race Mathews to me, 25 June 2015.

72   "As right-wing": *Age*, 22 April 1985, p. 1.

73   "His opponents use": *Australian Financial Review*, 18 March 2006, p. 26.

74   "They were the": Shorten to me, 30 July 2015.

74   "If the NUW": *Age*, 8 July 2000, p. 9.

76   "We recognise unions": *Age*, 20 July 2001, p. 3.

76   "How about simply": *Age*, 21 July 2001, p. 6.

77   "His flag is": *Crikey*, 4 June 2002, www.crikey.com. au/2002/05/26/delia-delegate-dishes-dirt-doozies/?wpmp_switcher=mobile&wpmp_tp=4.

77   "When I first": Latham, *The Latham Diaries*, p. 297.

77–8   "I said that": Latham, *The Latham Diaries*, p. 318.

78   "The key challenge": *Australian*, 21 July 2004, p. 15.

78–9   "Yet the Howard" and "There is a problem": Shorten, address to the National Press Club, 27 February 2002.

80   "Labor's task now": *Arena*, 1 December 2004, www. thefreelibrary.com/The+new+centre.-a0126787732.

80   "absolute horseshit": Latham, *The Latham Diaries*, p. 14.

81   "a magnificent achievement": *Age*, 13 February 2004, p. 2.

82   "The resulting alliance": *Australian*, 26 November 2005, p. 23.

83   "I do think": *Australian*, 6 June 2005, p. 2.

83   "There are no": Greg Combet to me, 25 August 2015.

83–4   "It throws up" and "you cannot get": Gerry Kitchener to me, 24 June 2015.

84–5   "What is democratic": *Age*, 19 March 2005, p. 3.

85   "I'm not going": *Age*, 16 March 2005, p. 3.

85–6   "Richard Marles explained": *Australian*, 26 January 2006, p. 2.

87–8   "I've done everything": *Australian*, 15 March 2006, p. 2.

89   "one of our thinkers": *Australian*, 24 October 2005, p. 2.

89   "a branch-stacking oaf": *Crikey*, 26 May 2002.

90   "To continually promote" and "He is the next": *Sunday Age*, 21 June 2015, p. 7.

91   "We haven't won": Campaign letter, *Age*, 4 February 2006, p. 6.

91   "The OC notes": *The Other Cheek*, 27 August 2005, http://pandora.nla.gov.au/pan/64343/20061130-0000/andrewlanderyou.blogspot.com/2005_08_27_andrewlanderyou_archive.html.

92   "Sercs made an": Andrew Landeryou, 28 July 2005, http://pandora.nla.gov.au/pan/64343/20061130-0000/andrewlanderyou.blogspot.com/2005_07_28_andrewlanderyou_archive.html.

92   "He's hard-working": *Age*, 4 February 2006, p. 6.

92   "The old saying": *Australian*, 19 August 2005, p. 7.

93   "The central problem": *Australian Financial Review*, 7 February 2006, p. 53.

93   "He's not the": *Australian*, 22 February 2006, p. 1.

96   "He's a capable": *Mercury*, 13 May 2006, p. 3.

97   "He wants to be PM": Information to me.

97   "Bill Shorten likes": "Insight", *Age*, 12 November 2005, p. 3.

98   "It really drives": Information to me.

101   "Bill for PM": *Daily Telegraph*, 16 May 2006, p. 1.

101   "throwing a Kleenex": *Canberra Times*, 10 May 2006, p. 2.

102   "that you continue": Tony Wright, *Bad Ground*, 2009, p. 287.

102   "We cannot afford": *Sydney Morning Herald*, 11 May 2006, p. 15.

Sources

102   "He gave, too": Bob Ellis, *And So It Went*, Penguin, 2009, p. 214.

102–3   Leadership support: ACNielsen Poll, 21 May 2006.

103   "to ring me": *Australian*, 17 May 2006, p. 2.

103   "Maribyrnong was what": Shorten's testimony, 8 July 2015, p. 6.

104   "The AWU was": Shorten's testimony, 8 July 2015, p. 26.

104   "re-emerged as an": *Australian*, 1 March 2006, p. 6.

104   "Unions can waste": *Australian Financial Review*, 25 September 2007, p. 1.

105   "Mr Shorten said": *Australian Financial Review*, 16 November 2006, p. 3.

105   "Ted, would you", "a bit of" and "a good cut": Shorten's testimony, 8 July 2015, pp. 22, 30 & 11.

106   "The idea that": Shorten's testimony, 8 July 2015, p. 25.

106   "He was a": Shorten's testimony, 8 July 2015, p. 6.

106   "When you're the": Shorten's testimony, 8 July 2015, p. 33.

107   "You will have": Shorten's testimony, 8 July 2015, p. 73.

107   "At the National": Shorten's testimony, 8 July 2015, p. 74.

107–8   "I can just": Shorten's testimony, 8 July 2015, p. 72.

108–9   "On the boards": *Hansard*, 14 February 2008, p. 328.

109   "I will be leading": *Australian*, 5 December 2006, p. 1.

110   "We've fixed Bill": Information to me.

110   "If you want" and 'This is going": Kelty to me, 22 July 2015.

110   "He just didn't": Information to me.

111   "People give you": *Sunday Age*, 23 November 2008, p. 21.

111   "It's nothing to": *Sunday Times* (Perth), 16 June 2013, p. 67.

111–12 "In the evening": *Courier-Mail*, 5 September 2007, p. 78.

112   "That's plain wrong": Shorten to me, 13 January 2016.

112   "I believe in God", etc.: Shorten to me, 30 July 2015.

Sources

113–14 "It was at the heart" and "When I hear": Shorten, speech to the Australian Christian Lobby, 25 October 2014, www.alp.org.au/shorten_acl_address.

114–15 "It is a bit": *Australian*, 20 January 2009, p. 5.

115 "Parliament was sitting": Kitchener to me, 24 June 2015.

115 "He actually fell": Gillard, *My Story*, p. 418.

116 "I wished the": *Age*, 4 May 2013, p. 5.

116 "That is what": *Australian Financial Review*, 15 February 2010, p. 60.

117–18 "Shorten makes no": Wikileaks, 12 June 2009, wikileaks.org/plusd/cables/ 09MELBOURNE69_a.html.

118 "That's what it's": Information to me.

119 "the last practical": *Sydney Morning Herald*, 24 November 2009, p. 4.

119 "in electoral trouble": Paul Kelly, *Triumph and Demise*, MUP, 2014, p. 10.

119 "We had to do": Shorten, on *Q&A*, ABC TV, 28 June 2010.

120 "He was dismayed": Barrie Cassidy, *The Party Thieves*, MUP, pp. 81–2.

120 "should think about this": Shorten, on *Q&A*, ABC TV, 28 June 2010.

121 "We're bloody stuffed": Sam Dastyari, *The Killing Season*, ABC TV, 16 June 2015.

121 "It was spontaneous": Kelly, *Triumph and Demise*, p. 10.

121 "I honestly don't": Kitchener to me, 24 June 2015.

122 "Don't mistake this": Information to me.

122 "infamous footage": Shorten to me, 30 July 2015.

122 "I am now advised": Kelly, *Triumph and Demise*, p. 326.

123 "Shorten was in": Kitchener, *The Killing Season*, ABC TV, 16 June 2015.

123 "He was still": Kitchener to me, 24 June 2015.

123 "He said you couldn't": Kitchener, *The Killing Season*.

Sources

126   "She wasn't one": Kitchener to me, 24 June 2015.

127   "The five peak": Rob Oakeshott, *The Independent Member for Lyne*, Allen & Unwin, 2014, p. 290.

127   "This week the": *Australian*, 17 December 2010, p. 12.

127–8   "Shorten brings to": Paul Barry, *Power Index*, www. thepowerindex.com.au/politicians/bill-shorten-power-index, 24 April 2012.

129   "I don't believe": *Australian*, 13 December 2011, p. 6.

129   "the union fox": *Australian Financial Review*, 13 December 2011, p. 1.

129–30 "This *fucking* language": www.youtube.com/ watch?v=RkKTI_PHpjI.

130   "I support the": *Q&A*, ABC TV, 20 February 2012.

131   "Life's a journey": *Sunday Herald Sun*, 13 May 2012, p. 4.

131   "These matters are": *Age*, 27 April 2012, p. 1.

132   "Do you think": *Australian*, 27 April 2012, p. 13.

132   "Is Bill Shorten": *Guardian*, 27 April 2012, www. theguardian.com/world/shortcuts/2012/apr/27/bill-shorten-loyal-politician-australian.

132   "Shorten was clearly": *Sun Herald*, 29 April 2012, p. 81.

134   "a cheap political": *Age*, 27 April 2012, p. 2.

134   "I can't vote" etc.: *Australian Financial Review*, 21 June 212, p. 1.

135   "I know the": *Australian Financial Review*, 22 June 2012, p. 1.

135–6   "That account was": *Lateline*, ABC TV, 21 November 2012.

137   "It's been a big": *Age*, 22 March 2013, p. 2.

138   "When governments are": Information to me.

139   "I support her": *Daily Telegraph*, 13 June 2013, p. 1.

140   "I hoped that": Shorten to me, 30 July 2015.

140–1 "Shorten wanted to" Kelly, *Triumph and Demise*, p. 468.

141   "I have now": *Australian Financial Review*, 27 June 2013, p. 8.

Sources

141 "Because that's not": Shorten to me, 30 July 2015.

144–6 "for sensible reasons" and all other quotes: Dyson Heydon, Reasons for Ruling on Disqualification Applications, 31 August 2015.

147 "Everything the royal": *Australian*, 1 September 2015, p. 1.

150 "We do retain": *Australian Financial Review*, 9 September 2013, p. 13.

150 "It's very hard": Information to me.

151 "Bill will get": *Australian Financial Review*, 12 September 2013, p. 1.

151 "The mechanisms": *Herald Sun*, 9 July 2013, p. 6.

152 "out Albo-ing": *Australian*, 28 September 2013, p. 8.

152 "If I was to": *Sydney Morning Herald*, 25 September 2013, p. 8.

152 "We like what": *Australian*, 1 October 2013, p. 4.

152 "They broke arms": Information to me.

153 "did things to" and "You probably get": This post was captured in a screengrab at https://kangaroocourtofaustralia. files.wordpress.com/2013/11/bill-shorten-rape-2-edited.jpg.

154 "I assisted Kathy": Larry Pickering, "I was raped by Bill Shorten", 16 September 2014, http://pickeringpost.com/ story/-i-was-raped-by-bill-shorten-cont-/3803.

154 "Lawyers for the": *Australian*, 14 November 2013, p. 1.

155–7 "I feel loss" and "She believed in": Notes from Shorten's eulogy for his mother, delivered 15 April 2014, supplied by Shorten.

156 "He did the" and "a very emotional": Brennan to me, 22 August 2015.

157 "I thought my": *Kitchen Cabinet*, ABC TV, 4 November 2014.

158 "At the end": *Sunday Herald Sun*, 9 August 2015, p. 27.

158 "There was no" and "How am I": *Australian*, 21 August 2014, p. 3.

194

Sources

158–9 "I fully co-operated": Fragmented reports of his statement and answers – *Age*, 22 August 2014, p. 4; *Australian*, 22 August 2014, p. 2; *Herald Sun*, 4 October 2014, p. 2.

160 "That smirking phoney": *Hansard*, 19 August 2015, pp. 47–8.

160 "a sombre mood": Andrew Catsaras, 21 August 2015, http://andrewcatsaras.blogspot.com.au.

161–3 "I know there is" etc.: Shorten to me, 30 July 2015.

164 "We were right": *Hansard*, 14 July 2014, p. 7697.

164 "For Labor": *Hansard*, 1 September 2014, p. 9148.

166 "If you're going": *Australian Financial Review*, 29 August 2015, p. 4.

166 "one of the": *New Matilda*, 30 August 2015.

166 "The beauty of being leader": *Sydney Morning Herald*, 10 April 2010.

167 "reactionary, fractured" and "Last night": *Hansard*, 15 September 2015, p. 10,234.

170–1 "God will damn" and all quotes from the Why Knot forum, www.theguardian.com/australia-news/audio/2016/apr/04/why-knot-a-spirited-discussion-about-marriage-equality-in-full-audio.

172 "But I didn't predict": Shorten to me, 7 April 2016.

172 "politically motivated royal": *Australian*, 7 November 2015.

172 "Labor does have": Shorten, press conference, 7 December 2015, www.billshorten.com.au/press-conference-melbourne-labors-plan-to-strengthen-accountability-and-transparency-of-unions-governments-innovation-statement.

172–3 "louts, thugs, bullies": Heydon's final report, vol. 1, par. 10.

173 "When several of these themes": Heydon's final report, vol. 1, par. 68.

174 "High protein, low carbs" etc.: Shorten to me, 7 April 2016.

174 "I believe it's important": Shorten, press conference, 11 January 2016, www.billshorten.com.au/doorstop-

queanbeyan-malcolm-turnbulls-15-per-cent-gst-on-everything-liberal-partys-trade-union-royal-commission.

175–7   "I thought that" etc.: Shorten to me, 7 April 2016.

177–8   "I'm a unionist": Shorten, address to the National Press Club, 15 March 2016, www.billshorten.com.au/q_a_national_press_club_tuesday_15_march_2016.

179–80 "I look forward": Shorten to me, 15 September 2015.